Daydreaming in Spanglish

Raquel Polanco

Daydreaming in Spanglish
Written by: Raquel Polanco

Published by Voices Publishing

Front cover design by Kara Nieuwsma
Copy editing by Casselberry Creative Design

This book or parts thereof may not be reproduced in any form, stored in a retrieval system, or transmitted in any form by any means--electronic, mechanical, photocopy, recording, or otherwise--without prior written permission of the publisher, except as provided by United States of America copyright law.

Copyright 2021 by Raquel Polanco.

All rights reserved.
ISBN 9798710733714

*For the ones who never sleep
and the ones who dream with their eyes wide open.*

SLEEP CYCLE FOR DREAMERS

reverie
1. Morir Soñando — 19
2. Brown Sugar, Canela, And Latin American Spice — 20
3. Three Church Girls — 21
4. Honduran Rivers — 22
5. Semantics — 23
6. Blended Cultures — 24
7. La Hermandad — 25
8. Mechanic — 26
9. Piel Color A Miel — 27
10. For Empaths — 29
11. Faldas — 30
12. Crescent — 31
13. Dear Curvy Girl — 32
14. Poetry — 33
15. Holy — 34
16. Growing Up Bilingual — 35
17. Sweet Daughter — 36
18. Staying Gold — 37
19. Brown Skin Girl — 38
20. Architecture — 39
21. Gold — 40
22. a daydream — 41
23. She Knew She Found Her Tribe — 42
24. Para La Vecina Que Regala Una Taza De Azúcar — 43
25. Eden And Garden Snakes — 45
26. Tradition — 46
27. A Poem For My Mother — 47
28. Terms Of Endearment — 51
29. When The Joke Doesn't Translate Well — 52
30. Star Sailor — 53
31. She Has Learned To Travel Light — 54

32.	Stethoscope	55
33.	The Transcendentalists	56
34.	The Romantics	57
35.	Flowers In Her Hair	58
36.	Soloist	59
37.	I Come From	60
38.	Spanglish	61

rem

39.	There's Not A Word For That In English	64
40.	Call Me By My Name	65
41.	In Order	70
42.	In The Same Breath	72
43.	Airports, Borders, & Other Sources Of Creative Freedom	73
44.	Then, God Made Woman	74
45.	For Survivors Healing In Doses	75
46.	Dear Brown Girl	76
47.	Birth	77
48.	Staring Contest	78
49.	Dear Female	79
50.	Magic Body	80
51.	All Caps	83
52.	Origami	84
53.	Sandcastles	86
54.	Tuesday	87
55.	Make Room	90
56.	Tissues	91
57.	Embroidery	93
58.	Master of Disguise	94
59.	743	95
60.	All In Our Feels With Not Enough Language	96
61.	Roses & Beauty That Influences Love	97
62.	For Curly Girl	99

64.	Goodbye	100
65.	By This Age	104
66.	For Soulmates	105
67.	"We Are Tired Of Being Beautiful. But No One Complains."	106
68.	A Couple Of Kids	108
69.	The Myths	109
70.	The Turning Tables	111
71.	For Insecure Girls	113
72.	Anything And Absolutely Everything	117
73.	For The Ones With Bullet Proof Chests	119
74.	Fluent	120
75.	Two Sides, Same Coin	121

recurring

76.	The Writer & Sweet Body	126
77.	My Vulnerability	131
78.	I Grew Up Barefoot	132
79.	Rearview Mirror	134
80.	Transported	135
81.	No Way To Love	137
82.	By The Time It Reached Her	138
83.	Comparing Thee To A Summer's Day	139
84.	Calling It Even	141
85.	Unlike Me, Yet Like Me	142
86.	Theoretically	143
87.	Cardiomyopathy	144
88.	Cardiac Arrest	145
89.	Silent Prayers	146
90.	Some Truths & A Lie	147
91.	Skeletal	149
92.	Atomic	150
93.	Rock Bottom	151
94.	For Heart-Sleeved Humans	152

95. Crying Over Spilled Tea	153
96. Heart Condition	154
97. 25th Hour	155
98. a daydream	156
99. The Turning Page	157
100. Honestly	158
101. Out Of The Blue	159
102. a daydream	161
103. The Other Side	162
104. Mad Hatter	163
105. Eye Of The Storm	164
106. I Don't Always Say "I love you"	165
107. Touring Musician	168
108. Dear Educated Girl	169
109. Treasure Map	170
110. Isn't It Funny	172
111. Groceries	174
112. Brown Girls In America Ask:	178
113. Dreamboat Means Translating Streams Of Consciousness	179

restlessness

115. Last Night	183
116. Pillow Fights	184
117. Body Language	185
118. Lovers	187
119. Another Word	188
120. a daydream	189
121. Restraining Order	190
122. Having People And Not Having People	191
123. All of Me	192
124. Deal	193
125. For Fighters Who Are Also Lovers	195

126. Howl	196
127. Whisper	197
128. Echo	198
129. Anchor	200
130. a daydream	201
131. Shadow	202
132. Accents	203
133. a daydream	204
134. Interrupted Sleep Patterns	205
135. Love And Civility	206
136. Aerial Somersaults	207
137. The Acrobat	208
138. Departure Gate	209
139. What They Both Agreed	210
140. Playing With Fire	212
141. a daydream	213
142. Bedside Manner	214
143. Shadow Puppet	215
144. Liminality	216
145. a daydream	217
146. Metaphors	218
147. Hyperbole	219
148. Rent	220
149. Conversations In The Shade	221
150. What Can Cure A Broken Heart?	222
151. Eternal Childhood Of An Escapist Mind	223
152. Dreamland	225
153. I Want To Reclaim Language	226
154. That Night	227

realized
155. Campfires & Storytelling	231
156. Corn, Cactus, Turtle	232
157. XYZ	236
158. Childhood Homes	237
159. Driving Lessons	238
160. Melanin	239
161. Roam And The American Passport	241
162. Margins	242
163. Divinity	243
164. Colocha	244
165. Past Tense	245
166. Surviving, Surviving	247
167. a daydream	248
168. Growth Spurt	249
169. Para Mis Abuelos	250
170. Writer's Block	252
171. Gravity	253
172. Make Poetry Great Again	254
173. We Spend So Much Time	258
174. No English Equivalent	259
175. Citing Sources	260
176. A Few Good Men	261
177. She Was The Type	263
178. a daydream	264
179. If People Were Poetry	265
180. Pelo Malo?	268
181. Undivided	269
182. I am	270
183. What If	271
184. Evolution of A Voice Box	272
185. Old Soul	277

187. Los Ancianos Soñarán Sueños   278
188. Fire Breather   279
189. Lessons My Curls Have Taught Me   281
190. Becoming   283
191. a daydream   284
192. Antepasados   285
193. Dream Recollection   286
194. The Greatest Gift   287
195. Arrugas & Grey Hair   288

a note from the author:

For as long as I can remember my parents have been telling me stories about our family, my identity, our culture, and the values that make us undeniably Hispanic. I have loved hearing every single one of these stories. My favorite nights are still the ones filled with storytelling, where we stay up late con una tasa de café and I get to listen to Abuela recount narratives about the days before I existed, while mami y papi correct her on the details. We laugh and I learn more and more about our family through their memories and the questions they answer. Most of my favorite stories take place years before my time when mami was still a young girl in Honduras and papi was somewhere in Bani with his eleven siblings still dreaming about America.

Ever since I was young, my parents did an exceptional job teaching me about who I am and letting me taste it in our food or learn about it through our language. I grew up only speaking Spanish until I was five. After that, the world became a maze which I navigated with two languages on my tongue: Spanish and English. I fell in love with language. By age seven I knew I had an affinity for words, and by age nine I knew I wanted to be a writer. I became a poet sometime in elementary school, and later in college I went on to major in English. I fell in love with literature. When reading about the Transcendentalists I was certain I had found my soulmates.

Over the years, Spanglish became the language I lived and breathed. People often ask me if I think in Spanish, since it's my first language, and the answer is always yes. Yes. I think in Spanish, I feel in Spanish, I worship in Spanish, and a part of me believes that my love language knows how to roll its R's. But the other side of this truth is that I also think, feel, worship, and love in English. The best way I can describe it would be a perfect blend of the two languages – what us second generation kids call:

Spanglish. This dichotomy is never something I think much about. I simply embody the duality of both languages and live in a way that keeps one foot in each world at all times. What W. E. B. Du Bois refers to as our "double consciousness" in his brilliant work, *The Souls of Black Folk*.

When I think about my upbringing – being fully Latina and being raised in America (in Alaska to be specific) – all I think about is how everything began with a dream. *Daydreaming in Spanglish* is a collection of poetry about identity, home, and the essence of code-switching. In these pages I honor my parents, expose the fallacies of the American "dream," process heartache, share more about my culture, and depict the intricacies of being a Hispanic-American female. This book you hold in your hands is itself a realized dream. Poetry is, for me, the sacred path towards healing and empathy thus I hope through my storytelling we can feel more connected and understood. I also pray I do our stories justice. In these poems I bear witness.

Welcome to my world of daydreams, where I live and love in two distinct languages.

rev·er·ie

/ˈrev(ə)rē/

noun
a state of dreamy meditation; a daydream

Morir Soñando
popular beverage of the Dominican Republic usually made with orange juice, milk, cane sugar or vanilla extract, and chopped ice

When you are a "second generation" kid,

Being raised in 21 Century America,

You learn to speak in English,

But you never stop dreaming in Spanish

Brown Sugar, Canela, And Latin American Spice

Celia Cruz coined her catchphrase "¡*Azúcar!*"
As an acknowledgement and celebration of Latinx culture and tradition
As well as a "battle cry" and tribute to the African slaves who worked in Cuba's sugar plantations
¡*Azúcar!* is Spanish for *Sugar!*

Mami raised my sisters and me to believe we were made of brown sugar, canela, and everything nice
So naturally.. I put azúcar in everything!

Azúcar, to sweeten my tea
Azúcar, to create my natural face scrubs
Azúcar, para preparar the perfect glass of Morir Soñando or cafecito con leche

Three Church Girls

Swaying in the church

To the rhythm of my roots

We walked into the temple

Towards the throne room

Barefoot

No carpet

No tile

Just floor

And we danced

As the soil broke against our calloused heels

We yielded ourselves to the Father and let His Spirit break

our calloused hearts

Honduran Rivers

Rushing to the river with mamá

She taught us to wash our clothes and drown our fears in

river water

Soap suds surrounding our feet

As we scrubbed and we bathed

Kneeling, we twisted droplets of hard labor from the clothes

on our backs

Mud sticking to our feet on the walk back home

El Barrio de mi niñez

Racing to the roof

Where we'd hang our clothes to bask in the sun

That knew us by name.

Immigrant

Is

Just

A

Fancy

Word

For

Dreamer

Blended Cultures

You can stare at a girl for hours

And never really see her

You can read her poetry out loud

And never know the sound of her voice

You can mispronounce her name

And still fall in love with the way her name rolls off the tongue

She can introduce herself

Without an accent on her lips

And her voice may drip America

But she will always be Latinoamérica

Her mind will know it

Her body will remember

Her heart will yearn for

Homelands made of fire

Built on beauty and rememory.

La Hermandad
for my sisters

Dear Sisters,

There's nothing I've loved more than being your middle

Because sleeping in the center of our bottom bunk bed

And sliding into the middle seat of Mami and Papi's van

And being squeezed while sharing a room with each of you

At different times in our lives

Has perfectly positioned me to feel your love.

and ultimately, with us, love is the thing that we do best

                                                          Love, R

                                      Forever your center console

She's a lousy mechanic

But she's never been afraid to get her hands dirty

If it meant she could fix whatever

Heart valve had been broken

Piel Color A Miel

I always wanted skin like my mother's

Glowy

Smooth

And fair

Skin

Mirror mirror on the wall,

Who's the fairest of them all?

For me the answer was always my mother

For years it was her complexion I desired

I watched her

Brush her beautiful dark hair

Decorate her porcelain skin

Painting with cosmetics

As I watched

Sitting on her lap

I admired her.

She accentuated every feature on her face

Already beautiful to me,

Taking her time

With every brushstroke

Revealing to me her secrets.

She is both Michelangelo

And the Sistine Chapel:

God reaching for man
Finding woman first
Heaven touching earth

I wanted to be just like her

My father, the color of coffee
My mother, the cream to his coffee
My sisters and I
The brown sugar
The honey
The sweetener
To their cup of blended brown love

She liked talking about feelings

Because somewhere, someone

had made empathy her first language.

Faldas

Our hips bloomed like roses

Our grandmothers gardened with

Far before we were to know anything

about birds, bees, and pollination.

Crescent
for the ones who remain whole even when feeling less than full

Learning to love ourselves

In the in-between stages

We are the moon

existing in phases.

Dear Curvy Girl,

You are gorgeous girl. You are often also hungry girl and insecure girl. But I need you to love yourself girl. Be working out because you love yourself girl. And not for any other reason. Embrace the bones that God designed to build your structure in and love the hips that are gifts from your mother. And her mother before her. Never punish yourself for your appetite. This world has taken so much from you it's no mistake you want to fill yourself. Take it back. But curvy girl protect yourself. Do not let them reduce you to pieces of your body. You are not just your frame. You are not their symbol. You are limb and bruises but also you are beauty, in busy Nuyorican buildings. Build yourself and your body. Love her, your body, kiss her and treat her well. Because you are these bones you're made of so I pray you let yourself be unbreakable.

Yours truly

Poetry

Isn't about pen and paper

It is about words and the poet.

Like all art,

Poetry becomes the art of soul alchemy.

It takes the form of sorcery

in the way poets become

the sounding board for pain

Absorbing the blow one way

And distilling sonnets birthed from suffering

In the opposite direction.

Stringing together sentences made out of sorrow

Reimagine how poets become meaning makers and

Poetry writing emerges as the subtle art of bracing for impact.

Holy

I want to turn my love for you
Into an everyday habit.

I want to break down my lifestyle
Into weekly routines we've built around each other.

I want transform the art of loving you
Into holy rituals we deem sacred.

Growing Up Bilingual

Means you think in two languages.

You learn to push past accents

All the while coveting accents

Because you want to hear what the person is saying

And sovereignly know the accent is saying something too

Growing up bilingual

Means feeling something twice

Being fluent in flowing

Learning in two modes

Switching codes so naturally

It becomes second nature

Two languages

Become second nature

Spanish or English

Neither a second language

Both a blend of beautiful

Spanglish, the love language

Of third culture kids like me.

Sweet Daughter

we are not disempowered

because someone else

is empowered

Staying Gold

Mix star dust with earth

and watch it turn to gold

these are the ones

we call people of color

Brown Skin Girl

Some days I want to love America

But most days it feels she cannot bear to love me back

Perhaps she has lost the courage to even try

Architecture

We are magic in human form.

Cathedrals made of flesh.

Metaphors deeply begging to be understood.

Gold

I didn't know something could break so beautifully

Who knew after all that fire

You'd break a heart

Wide open

& all that would be left

Is gold

solid gold.

How many metaphors do we miss in a lifetime because we're all out of words?

How many sentiments are we unable to convey because we lack the language to express emotions?

She knew she found her tribe

anytime she introduced herself in Spanish

Para La Vecina Que Regala Una Taza De Azúcar
for the nextdoor neighbor who lends a cup of sugar

Ayuda

A simple word

¿Ayúdame?

An uncomplicated question

Yet when we use it

How we use it

Where we use it

And towards who

Can mean so much.

Amongst immigrants *ayuda* is often

The most important

Most common

Most useful word

On our lips.

When spoken

and reciprocated

It is the feeling of a kiss.

Belonging exchanged

Between friends

Becoming family.

Ayuda:

A simple word

That forges families

Out of communities

Who hold this word in common

Sharing it on our tongues

We pass it down like recipes,

like family secrets.

Eden And Garden Snakes

Who told us

we were not enough?

Who told us we needed to be brilliant to be like God?

Who force fed us the lie that being brown,

being made of earth's melanated dust,

was not godliness enough?

Tradition

Mami and Papi always say:
Anyone who wants to date you,
must come to the house and ask for permission before taking you out
Así son las cosas
There is curfew as long as you live with us,
Porque a ti no se te ha perdido nada ahí afuera en la calle
This is the way
Whenever you see us, or an elder, for the first time, siempre pídan la bendición
That is tradition

Siempre saluden con un beso y un abrazo
Donde quiera que vayan, si hay visitas, siempre saluden
Pídanle a la gente si quieren café
Aprendan a consinar
Aqui, todo los dias se limpia
Traeme la chancleta
Never talk back
Always know your place
Respect your elders
Cuando respondan digan "mande"
Digan buen provecho cuando alguien está comiendo
Siempre oren antes de comer, al despertar, y acostar
Cuidense la una a la otra
Take care of each other

Así son las cosas
This is the way

That is tradition.

A Poem For My Mother

I want to meet the teenage version of my mother
I want to know her
Before she was somebody's wife
Before she was anyone's mother
Before she was my mother
Before I knew her as *mine*
I wish I knew her when she was still *hers*
All her own
Belonging to no one, but herself.
I wish I knew her then
I think we may have been friends.
Did she have as many questions then
As I do now?
What were her questions? Her doubts? Her fears or apprehensions?
Who answered her questions?
Taught her not to be afraid of the dark, or the wild, or of men
Who told her she was a daughter of the Nile?

How did she spend her nights, her mornings, and her internal rainy days?

What was her love language?
Who did she love before she met my father
What did she know about heartbreak?
Were her tears and her process anything like mine?

Who consoled her?
Who did she trust?
Who didn't she trust?
Why not?

What happened to her in the days before she became my hero,
When no one was around to save her?

How did she teach herself the things she teaches me now?

All the things she seems so sure of.
The virtues, results, and effects of her experiences.
What were her experiences?
Who did she laugh with? and what about?
With whom did she share a thousand cups of coffee before I came along and she poured them for me?
Who walked her home from school?
How did she spend her money? Her time?
What .. and who.. did she invest in?
What mattered most to her and why?
What was her favorite snack and why?
Her guilty pleasure and why?

What stole her attention in the days, months, years, before she had me?
What set her soul on fire? What stressed her out?
How is she so beautiful?
Was she still so lovely whenever she was angry? Or defensive? Or resentful?
Who was the first person her bitterness was directed towards?
Or the first person who broke her trust?
What happened then? How did she feel? Did she recover? If so, how?
Did she forgive them? If yes, how?
Has forgiveness always felt so natural or been so instinctual for her?
How?

What makes her so determined?
Are the answers to these questions the reasons she seems so indestructible now?
I met her whole.
But where did she learn how to self-soothe?
How to build a body that could never be broken?
How to be the sort of person that could heal herself...
Over
    and
        over

           again
                    at the expense of no one else

I know she was a victim,
but by the time I met her,
she was already full fledged survivor
Pledged with warrior women,
Who came before her.

Who taught her how to say yes? How to say no?
How to think for herself?
Fearlessness and yet, how to hide so well from others?
What was her relationship with her father?

What was her relationship with makeup?
She knows her face so well and can decorate each detail of her face without a mirror.
She is divine.
Was she ever as insecure as I am?
Who was the first person to tell her that she is beautiful? Did she believe them?
How long before she knew it for herself? When did she discover she was exquisite?
How did she uncover this? In that exact moment, how did she feel?

What secrets is she still keeping?
& for who?
Why still keep them?
What is she keeping safe?
Before me, who did she love enough to protect?

Was she happy then? As happy as the day she met me?
When I became hers and, for the first time, I knew her as mine.

She is so full of life
and loss and the lessons her mistakes must have taught her.

I am flesh of her flesh, yet how much of her do I carry in my bones?

I want to meet the teenage version of my mother.
I want to understand what's hidden within the reservoirs of her memory,
My fire breathing mother
who taught me about oceans
Told me I was one of them
Taught me how to cross rivers
with my bare feet.
Wash my clothes in them too and taught me
How I myself am a body of water
With a fire beneath my belly
That grumbles and echoes with stories of women
just.
like.
Her.

Bone of her bone, I am the version of her she never expected
She is made and remade in me
And we meet and re-meet in each other.

Her eyes
My smile
Her character
My will
My face, cupped
In her hands
I see the teenage version of my mother.
She is the same fire. The same resistance. The same rebellion
And I am sure of her.

Terms of Endearment

Where I come from,
We use physical features
Like the color of one's skin
To create terms of endearment
For the ones we love

Everyone becomes:
Prieto
Mi negra
Moreno
Mi mulatica bella
Negrita
… and so on

And honestly, the pigment of your skin does not always matter
As my family members, with fairer skin, are often referred to in the same manner

Put simply,
Where I come from
Melanin is beautiful
And we celebrate our color
Through our expressions of love

When The Joke Doesn't Translate Well

There is so much I wish that I could tell you

So much I want to include you in

but language acts as a barrier

or a border that neither one of us can seem to cross.

Star Sailor

She is a voyager, exploring the confines of her own being
filled with wide-eyed wonder and
optimistic expectancy for what she may uncover on her
journey. She is soul searcher, finding
herself. A traveler, leading the expedition in her own time
and space between former self and
present being. She is navigator, sailing her way through the
waves of wandering who she is,
who she is expected to be, and who she is willing to become.
She is fluent in freedom and
fully self-aware of her connection with the land.
She is exploring solely for the sake of her self-discovery.
She is exploradora: anchored in the Truth and captivated by
the Way.

She Has Learned to Travel Light

but just because she can hold

all her emotional baggage,

on her own,

does not mean it is not heavy.

Stethoscope

She told him how her heart hurt

So he turned himself into a stethoscope

and until that moment, she had never known love

quite like this.

Lets

live

the

sort

of

lives

the

transcendentalists

told

stories

of.

Lets

be

the

sort

of

lovers

the

romantics

write

poetry

about.

Flowers in her hair, paper plane in hand, grass between her toes, this is how one would describe her.

She is gazing at the clouds, imagination already lost in another world of hers: her day dream within a day dream.

Breaking her concentration, only once, looking over at the trees deciding which one she will climb up next.

Soloist

She fine tuned her heart strings
Until he could no longer strum them.

She reminded herself she is string instrument
And not percussion on someone else's drumline.
She is more than snare and cymbals
for him to ensnare her with his symbolic romanticism.

She is magic made music
Her wildest memories tell tales of alchemist women who turned their
Brass hearts into string instruments made of Holy Rosaries
For men like him to cast their pagan prayers on.

Daughter of chemist composers,
She trained herself to be transformative
To be first fiddle
To love the tune of soloist songs and tap-dance relentlessly
to silent symphonies which emerge as a result of
philharmonics coming to a deafening end,
vamping till ready..
A haunted orchestra cuing the soloist as she enters
Her spirit a melodious sonnet of stillness and silhouette
heartstrings strumming effortlessly
To an anthem that needs no accompaniment.

I Come From

A family of poets and teachers

Dreamers and farmers

People who work with their hands

And dream with their eyes wide open

We are the ones with

Hearts so big conquistadores

Could never conquer.

Spanglish

The

language

of

two

homes,

a

split

psyche,

a

culture

within

a

culture,

The

merging

of

two

worlds.

rem

/ˈrem/

noun
the portion of deep sleep wherein dreams occur

There's Not A Word For That In English

Every now and then
Someone will say a word or express a feeling in English and I
will think to myself:
"There's a word for that in Latin…"
Or Peruvian
Or French
Or some other foreign language

Language. It is our culture

It holds our hands
carries us through everything Language forms
our identity Shapes our thoughts
Language is the making of meaning and meaning
making is a product of the collective

When I can't find the right word in the wrong language
When you ask me to be less than who I feel I am
It feels…
Well there's a word for that too,
But I can't find the translation.

I want to be like the word *Hallelujah*
understood by every culture
& fluent in every language

Call Me By My Name

When I was eleven months old I uttered my first word:
"papa"
Father in Spanish
Spanish, the language of my father and mother
And their fathers and mothers before them
O sea, mi abuela, bisabuela, y tatarabuela

I uttered my first word in Spanish because it is, to this day, my first language
First meaning primary
Meaning instinct
Meaning most natural
Most comfortable
Meaning in the beginning
Meaning en el principio God created the heavens and the earth
Meaning Spanish was the first language I ever learned about God in

My mother the worshiper sung hymns in Spanish to me as I laid still tucked within the
comfort and safety of her womb
My father whispering "el padre nuestro" in my ear as I repeated after him:
"padre nuestro que estás en los cielos santificado sea tu nombre" — the Lord's prayer
It was in spanish that I learned to pray
Spanish, meaning the language I learned to talk to God in
Meaning the only language I know to use to get an answered prayer

I was 11 months old when I spoke my first words: "papa"
& a couple of days later I spoke my second *"carrrro"*
Which is car in Spanish
So I learned it as *carrrro*
It was spanish, the first language I learned to laugh in
When friends & family would come over

my parents would bring me out and
Ask me to say *carro*, say *perro*
Trying to get me to say any word that would show how proud I was to be who I was
& to come from where we came from

But my favorite was always when someone would ask me my name
Proudly I would puff up my chest and wave the curls out of my face
Because my name was good
My name was great
My name is Raquel Carolina Polanco Cerrato
And trust me there were no R's left behind

And the adults they cheered and laughed and clapped and I felt good
Because my name was *mine* and it was *me* and it was something no one could ever take away
from me
Or so I thought

But of course, a few years later I started school
Imagine me, 5 years old, with an accent thicker than my curls
The teacher asks the students to introduce ourselves and tell the class "one fun thing about
yourself"

When it was my turn, I stood up
puffed up chest and brushed my curls away from my face
The only way I'd been taught how
But this time, the kids giggled
I could not name the feeling, but I knew then their laugh was not meant to be a compliment
Wasn't warm and welcoming like the laughs I get at home from my tíos and my tías

I questioned everything.
My name. My accent.

The R's that made up my name.
My favorite letter
And the inside joke I just seemingly told the class, but somehow missed...

Ashamed, I began to sit
but the teacher stopped me: "Wait, tell us, one fun thing about yourself"
I shook my head and sat
Thinking to myself: "I think I just told you"

Shakespeare asked, "What's in a name"
So cavalier and nonchalant as though its nothing
But I'll tell you that it's *everything*

"Okay thank you *RAW-KEL*" the teacher said to me

And I sat still

It was the first time I had heard anyone name me in English

That day I heard a lot of words but *the world* seemed foreign
Or I seemed foreign in it
I don't remember feeling like myself
Because I was Rrraquel
And this ra-quel person seemed like someone I didn't want to meet, let alone be
Throughout the day though
there was a lot of creativity
And I was named in many ways
I was named raw-quel, ro-quel, rachel, rochelle, someone even called me rebecca
With every mispronunciation
Pieces of me died inside
As the apostle whose name was changed from Saul to Paul
Or Abram to Abraham
Or Sarai to Sara
Or Jacob to Israel
I felt that I, too, was named by God

So what's in a name? *Everything*
Surely my name means *something*

But the problem must have been mine
Because after all I was the one with the "complicated" name, right?
After all, my name had an *r* and a *q* and these are complicated letters
That entire day, not a single person called me by my name

Afterschool I walked outside and heard my older sister call to me in Spanish
And I exhaled the deepest sigh
Unaware I had been holding my breath the entire day
We waited together for mama to pick us up
Who I couldn't wait to see
I just wanted to hear her say my name
In a language I was used to
With her familiar-motherly tone
In that way that only she could

She asked me about my first day and it took everything in me not to cry

I think she knew
I mean, her name is *Sara Del-Carmen*, so of course she knew

She cupped my face in her hands
And whispered our favorite saying,
"Mija, you are poetry in a world that is still learning the alphabet"

Except that she said it in Spanish:
The language I learned to pray to God in
The first language I fell in love in
The language I use to share secrets with my sisters
It is our family code

The language that connects me with a lineage of tíos, tías, abuelos, and abuelas
Who gave me a voice

As though we shared own little secret, mamá whispered to me in Spanish
The language of our God and answered prayers
The language that like a compass will always point us home
When she calls me by my name.

In

Order

To

Survive

We

Must

Learn

To

Be

Adaptable

In

Order

To

Be

Adaptable

We

Must

First

Be

Anchored

In The Same Breath

He told her she was beautiful
He reminded her that they lived in a world where
Her brown beauty could only be so beautiful.

"Your skin is so beautiful," he said,
"but I can't have any brown babies running around."

then without hesitation he leaned in and tried to kiss her.

Airports, Borders, & Other Sources of Creative Freedom

Whenever I cross a border I'm brown in a different way

Female in another form

Freed by the means of someone else's currency

Home or not home

I learn and relearn different ways of being brown,

I embody foreign and familiar ways of being female

beautiful

bicultural

and brown

because being melanated and being human

are not mutually exclusive.

Then, God made W O M A N

In the beginning female magic was formed.

Monday morning and she loves herself.
Reassures herself. She is her lovely self.
                                          IT IS GOOD.

Traumas triggered by Tuesday ..she now doubts herself.
                                          IT IS ALRIGHT.

Wednesday brings enough troubles of its own.
                                          IT IS NOT GOOD.
Thursday and she does not recognize God in her own mirror.
                      IT IS NOT GOOD FOR WOMAN TO BE ALONE.

5th day. . . . it's a humpback whale sweater sort of day.
She knows she is as sacred as
these goddesses of the sea.
                                          IT IS BETTER.

Saturday she remembers the image she is created in
Remembers how her body & complexion
are reflections of a timeless Deity.
                        IT IS AS DIVINE
                      AS SHE IS.
                                  On the seventh day, she rests.

For Survivors Healing In Doses

Isn't it tragic

How we can't escape the body

when it's experiencing pain?

Isn't it also divine

How the body

stores unimaginable trauma

and still survives?

Dear Brown Girl,

You have been switching codes for so long you forgot where to find the off mode. I want to know what your voice sounds like when you're not so busy editing yourself. Your melanin is not the problem. Brown skin is not a deadly sin. Dear Brown Girl you are also Afro-Latin Girl, you are Bi-Lingual girl, you are Spanish girl, you are Slam Poet girl, you talk a thousand miles a minute because you came from earth and star-dust when he took brown dirt to make Brown-Skin Girl, the world gave you too much to say in too little time. So your language is too fast track for their train of thoughts to keep up with. Your tongues got too much conga, too much cumbia, too much underground railroad to slow down. So set yourself free. When they ask you to sit still ask why. If they beg you to slow down, ask if they can listen faster. Acknowledge that when they ask you to switch codes, they are hijacking modes of being. Know their liberation is mutually bound up in yours so Brown Girl when they ask I pray you let yourself be fluent and free.

Truly yours

When they ask if I am the daughter of immigrants,

I will answer yes: I am the daughter of dreamers.

                                               Dreamers who give birth to poets.

Ever try to wish upon a star, but the constellations refuse to cooperate?

Dear Female,

You are not merely a girl. Do not allow anyone to reduce you to your former ages. You have worked hard to arrive. To be where you are. Where -- for the record -- they are too. You are more than your gender. Do not allow anyone, for any reason, ever to reduce your worth or your being to the anatomy of your body. Or your skin, your curls, your brains, your curves for that matter. Adichie said it best: "because you are a female" is never a reason for anything. Ever. Simply do not adhere to standards that are not your own or compromise your ethics, your tone, your message for someone else's commodity. Know you matter. Feel that truth to your very bones. And you will feel like you are taking up too much space, I guarantee you that you are not. I wish you'd let yourself be a nebula: the remnant of a supernova --holding together the remaining pieces of an exploding star that gave its life by splitting its light into the universe. Just be anything that they cannot eclipse. Dear Brown Girl, Dear Curly girl, Dear Smart Girl, Dear Curvy Girl, and Christian Girl don't forget to use your name. & it is okay to correct them when they get it wrong. Speak your name because it is your power. Your greatest form of consent. Your name is not a joke and your identity not the sum of all these monomers they see you as. You may be brown and curly, smart and curvy, charismatic and proud .. and yet, you are so much more than all these things. So be something that YOU'RE proud of. Be everything your grandmother made space for you to be. Just be anything but Quiet Girl.

Be Resurrected Girl

Be Realized-Dream Girl

Magic Body

It took me years to learn to love my body
Some days I am still learning how not to reject her
Most days I am still apologizing to her for treating her as more object than temple

It took me years to stop viewing my hips as an apology letter written to society
Though I'm sure when God made Eve he made her unapologetically

Most days I am still unlearning what the media taught me about my body
For years I saw my body as more theirs than mine
For years I watched the magic of my body unfold before our eyes
After all that is the trick right?
The pretty assistant is what the show is all about no?

You can bring a man on stage and call him a magician
& he can say he knows things. Has secrets he won't reveal
But it isn't really magic isn't until he brings her body up on stage and shows us how he can
literally saw her in half
And isn't *this* what the show is all about
Isn't this what we call magic
Isn't this the magic of her body
that she ever thought she might be in control at all
the real trick after all
That which entertains us
Vulnerable
Exposed
A show
Her body
We called it magic

the way a man saws a woman in half

And for a moment she feels beautiful
Because what men call beautiful is often magical
But to be called magic isn't always beautiful
When it requires our existence as the punchline to their joke
Demands our body as the trick for their magic
Makes our bodies a security blanket for their nightmares
Turns our dress code into reasons for their lack of discipline
Taking #MeToo out of context for the entertaining of their egos
Makes foolery of our wits by making us think that our bodies are all that's beautiful
That our bodies are all that's useful
That our magic is in our bodies
That our bodies are meant for carving
or show and telling
Choke and telling
Joke and telling
As though the last time he turned a woman into punchline was a joke worth telling

That our bodies!
Our bodies!!
Are for being torn apart
Limb from limb
Objectified
Piece by piece
compartmentalized
As though being a butt person is somehow better than being a boob person
Because they're still just pieces
Pieces of our bodies
Pieces of a whole
Being torn apart and viewed as fragments of a girl
A real girl
A whole girl
Human girl
Human

Do you know that I smile at every stranger that walks past me on the street hoping,
not that my hair flip might be mistaken as an imagined invitation,
but in the hopes that I might be seen as human
Fully human
Fully whole
Not parts of a show he was taught to use for entertainment
Or fragments of a magic trick he was taught to saw in half

It took me years to learn to love my body
Or better yet to unlearn everything the media taught me about my body
Let's just say,
I don't believe in magic anymore.

All Caps

She was the type of woman that would text in all caps.

Maybe because she never felt heard.

Origami

She learned to fold herself into origami for him
Made herself small for him
Small enough to fit into the cracks
And crevices of his life
Where he once held space for her
Refusing to make room for her
Leaving just enough room for her
To bend…
and she'd bend
So he'd never have to
break.

She learned to fold herself
into a million tiny creases

So that he wouldn't mind her margins
invading on his paper-thin patience.

and when that wasn't enough

She folded herself down further
into origami scraps for him
papier-mâchéd herself into
A thousand little love notes and played herself like an
origami orchestra for him,
but he couldn't hear her symphony.
He lacked the sympathy to know the sound of "I love you"
that she sung in reverse.
He was deaf to her melody.
She did not move him. She never reached him.

How could she?
Like every woman who has ever loved a man
She had mastered the art of becoming small for him Learned
to exist without being seen and without being heard Almost
invisible to his senses

She learned to fold herself into origami cranes for him
To fit inside his pocket
and she convinced herself
this could be enough.

Sandcastles

Our relationship was like building sandcastles.

We knew it wouldn't last forever,

yet we chose to turn each other into monuments

and dedicate time to what we knew had an expiration date.

What we knew from the beginning could not survive the tides

and would quickly wash away.

Tuesday

But even after everything I can't seem to stop hearing skinny as a compliment

On Tuesday I ran into an old friend, she told me I looked great.
Said that I looked skinny.

I hadn't lost any weight.. not recently, at least..
so I wondered if I was looking thinner due to stress

She said it'd been a year
She must have meant two because last year I was the thinnest I'd ever been.
See I'd just gotten my heart broken and had managed to convince myself that this too was
my fault. Somehow my eating habits and weight on a scale was the cause & effect for
someone else's lapse in judgement. Yea, I know. The logic right? But still, I thought...

Two years prior, however, I did weigh 45 pounds more than I do now and I was working hard
to lose the weight — the weight, mind you, that I had put on because of depression brought
on by a stressful first year in a predominantly-white institution and culturally eclectic new
city, but that must have been besides her point

She said I'd been " looking all...."

long pause

....Depressed?! I wanted to cut in and say

She never did finish that sentence
So I guess I'll never know what "all...." I was looking, but the entire time as my body was

paused waiting for an answer my mind was racing with all
the "all…." things I must have
been looking like:

All depressed
All insecure
All stressed
All sleep deprived
All hungry probably
Honestly
All malnourished
All I've skipped pretty much every meal this week except one
snack I might let myself have
daily and I still don't love myself
All I don't love myself
All self-hatred
All bad self-talk
All self-sabotage
All unhappy in my own skin
All miserable
All anxious
All counting calories
All pushing myself too hard on my workouts.. so hard I got
sick
All surviving strictly on vitamins and water I almost passed
out
All cutting everything out of my diet except water
All pretty… pretty sad
All thin & hollowed out
But she said skinny and I heard it as… pretty

You say skinny and I hear it as a compliment

I wanted to fill in the sentence but she said skinny
and everything stopped

Said skinny and I felt pretty
So I stopped

BUT SKINNY IS NOT SYNONYMOUS WITH PRETTY

In fact, I think my list was closer..

I want to untrain my poorly trained mind:
To stop hearing skinny as a compliment
To stop hearing skinny as synonymous with pretty
I want to aim for better
I want someone who hasn't seen me in a year to stop in the streets
       and say, "Wow! You're looking soooo.... *Healthy*!"

Make Room

Grief demands to be fully felt.

Let yourself be affected so you can learn.

So often crying is the entity that makes room for clarity.

Tissues

I no longer hand people tissues when they cry
I do not believe their pain
Or the expressing of their pain
To be problematic

Their process is exactly that:
A process ...fully theirs
One which deserves utmost respect
Without shaming
Or silencing
I bear witness to pain without having to fix it

I do not blame their pain
for my feeling uncomfortable

I choose to not be uncomfortable
Decide to find comfort in our mutual feelings of distress
In this shared experience
I am no longer uncomfortable

I sit with.
I hold space.
I remember pain as the most intrinsic virtue of the human experience
Our bodies hold these memories

There is no solution or easy fix
Thus, I do not offer temporary solutions in the form of tissue paper
I no longer ask the hurting to wipe away their hurt
The tangible tears
The proof of their pain
And their processing of that pain

Not for my benefit and certainly not for theirs
The only thing worse than denying personal pain
is dismissing someone else's

In these cases, the more we wipe away the less we cleanse
We are temples made of clay
Not doormats
No amount of sweeping under
Or swiping away tears serves us
Here, we heal from pain by exposing it

I no longer hand people tissues when they cry
I don't believe we should be wiping away our tears
Or trying to stop the crying

I believe our bodies are designed to feel
We are meant to let it out
Engineered to process
Suppression now the single greatest disillusion and greatest disservice of the human expression
Somewhere we learned that tears were made for tissues

Who told us that veiling away our pain would heal us any quicker?

Embroidery

It seems

No amount of sentences I string

together will ever be enough

To say I'm sorry

Not even "I love you"

Sung a thousand times

Into forever.

Master of Disguise

I always admired chameleons
For their camouflaging abilities
Here's a critter that can hide
And in doing so has mastered the art of self-preservation
I envied chameleons
Desired their intrinsic capabilities to be wired within my instincts too
What it must be like to stay safe and alive through the art of veiling?
Blending? Matching surroundings?

I later discovered that chameleons change color to reflect their moods
Sending social signals with their bodies
About their feelings
They communicate with other one another
The truth of their being

How I envied the lizards more now.
These reptilian creatures who knew more about feelings
Than a nine-year-old me
Who possessed more self-awareness than I held in the palm of my hand

The audacity of these highly evolved lizards
Teaching me truth through their emotional intelligence

I observed their instinctual emotional intelligence
Observed their expressing of moods
Observed their effective communication

This is how I learned they had, in fact,
mastered the art of self-preservation

743

She had no idea

a heart could love another human quite so much,

seven hundred and forty three poems worth to be exact.

All In Our Feels With Not Enough Language

How dare we tell our boys it's not okay to cry

Only to tell them otherwise

when they grow into men?

Roses and Beauty That Influences Love

The other day I saw a beautiful wildflower,
instinctively I went to touch it,
but its sharp and prickly thorns
drew my blood
and I thought about something my mother always says:
"Ella se defiende así sola"

Which is to say:
Beautiful things can also defend themselves

Which is *not* to say:
Beautiful things should have to defend themselves

Where did we learn that beautiful things desire our attention?

Where did we learn beauty was meant for touching?

Who do we think we are to assume beauty is meant for more than beholding?

Why do we assume beauty is to hands what flavor is to taste?

Where did we learn that in order to appreciate something beautiful we must also feel it?

When did feeling someone up become the best way to measure beauty?

When did we decide beauty would determine the worth of a woman?

The other day I saw a beautiful wildflower,
instinctively I went to touch it
but its sharp and prickly thorns
forced me to bleed

Perhaps because beauty is meant for admiring

not always for unveiling.

and while beauty wildly influences love,
the audacity of humanity
to ask a rose
to hide its thorns
so that we may never bleed
is tragically inhumane.

Dear Curly Girl,

You'll want to tame your locks so you can hide behind your skin.. Don't bother. There is no taming curls that are as wild as the jungle. They're made to match your wild heart and untamed tongue. You are rainforest made of moon vines. An amazon that cannot be braided back. Sis you are a whole vibe. And your hair a tribe of its own. A crown of curls I wish you'd let yourself be a wild dream. Curly girl accept that not accepting your hair is a losing battle. There is no use investing in relaxers, girl, your hair cannot relax. Think of it as therapy: as you work through every knot you can work out all your problems: Detangle, Let Go, Rinse, Repeat!

Yours truly

Goodbye

People say goodbye in many different ways
In various languages
And in countless other dialects

Sometimes goodbye sounds like
Adiós
Hasta luego
Ciao
Au revoir
Sayōnara
Aloha
Or Farewell

Other times goodbye is a phrase or an expression:
I can't do this anymore
I respectfully resign
Consider this my two-weeks' notice
I'm moving
Effective immediately
I need some space
A sticky note on the nightstand
I'm taking some time for myself
Lets just be friends
I don't love you anymore
A door slam
I love you
I'm sorry
I need to find myself
Tires screeching as the car drives off in the opposite direction
This isn't what I want anymore
A loved one getting smaller and smaller in the rearview mirror
You hang up first
A final breath
A last kiss
Take care of yourself
I hope you find what you are looking for

A plane departing
Another one landing
A box of mementos being handed back
A letter being left on the doorstep with no return address
You were the best thing that ever happened to me
I will always love you
A wave
A kiss blown with fingertips toward a lover's direction
A poem never intended to be read out loud
A side hug
Or the sort of hug that stops time for both of you
    As you can hear each other's heartbeats
        Feel each other's breath
            Smell each other's hair
A daydream
A fantasy you consider and never communicate
Another person
A Facebook status
A new haircut
An old engine refusing to start up again
I'm giving you your keys back
I never wanted this to happen
A graduation
A forehead kiss
Delete my number
A gunshot wound that never properly healed
A new city with a new zip code
A new phone with a new area code
The number you have dialed is no longer in service, please
hang up and try again
A fight between friends that was never reconciled
A long pause when they call to tell you you are loved,
                but you are too depressed to hear them
The use of a different pronoun
A ring left on a counter top after too many broken dishes after
too many broken promises
I'll miss you
Please do not speak to me ever again
A medical condition without a cure

A restraining order
Divorce papers
Emancipation papers
A death certificate
A death sentence
A glance across a crowded room
Hands pressed against the glass
We the jury, find the defendant, "guilty"
The look on your mother's face at the immigration office
Please take this time to say your goodbyes
Fingers reaching between wired fences
A fence you cannot hop
A bus headed back towards the border
Your back a bridge that can't bring them back
Cuidense mis hijos, el uno al otro
Tears and rage
Anger toward a system that forces too many unpleasant goodbyes
Te extraño
I'll always recognize you
I don't know you anymore
You've changed
A flag and a knock at the door
A weak apology
An email saying something about budget cuts
We regret to inform you…
At this time we will no longer be needing your services
We are ending our professional relationship
Game over
I hurt you
I didn't listen
I can no longer make time for this
A dropped call
An accident
An explosion
A lost connection
Tell the kids I love them and I'm sorry
You'll understand when you are older
I don't forgive you

It's not you it's me
Absence
Abandonment
I'm not sorry, I'm just done
It's over
The bell ringing
The book ending
The credits rolling
The crowd chanting "encore"
No one returning

Footsteps walking away
without a word

Silence always the loudest goodbye
Typically, also, the most effective.

By This Age

she still loved him,

but she had gained

too much self respect

to entertain his inconsistencies.

For Soulmates

There is a parallel universe where everything's sacred.

Where we took all the right turns
& missed none of the signs

And whatever universe that is
That is the one where my heart drums endlessly

with the version of you
that has married your soul with mine.

"We Are Tired of Being Beautiful. But No One Complains."
after Sandra Cisneros' The House on Mango Street

Man on the bus asks to look at me
I don't know this at first
When he taps me on the shoulder I think I must have
dropped something
I turn around
"I knew it," he says "You're beautiful.
I saw you when I came in thought you might be attractive,
but I couldn't really tell with a glance so I wanted to be sure.
Wow, yes. Let me look at you."
This one-sided conversation is lasting longer than I want it to
Quickly turning around
He taps me again
This time, I hardly glance over my shoulder
Headphone back in my ears
My music low because I am on high alert
I can still hear him:
"Oh come on honey, just let me look at you again. Let me just
look at you"

Except that you're not *just* looking.

This day. I am tired of being beautiful.
He calls me attractive, but at this moment I want nothing
more than to stop attracting.
Beautiful is not the word I would use to describe this feeling.
I feel small,
Used,
Underestimated,
And devalued
In the sort a way a flower must feel when it is plucked instead
of watered

Feeling unsafe
I count the stops it takes for me to arrive
31
To feel safe again

29
I enter The Grotto
Find a quiet place to rest
Hiding my face
I sit amongst the vines
And observe the roses
The roses with thorns
I only wish I had

Today, I was someone's "honey"
Tomorrow, I will be well-watered cactus.

A Couple of Kids

They knew each other for years

Loved each other for longer

But by the time they told each other

They only had days to hold each other

Days that turned to weeks

That turned right back to days

She pushed her flight back twice

not that it mattered

It was only a matter of time

They were running out of time

Like mad hatters,

Time a crazy thing

Even in wonderland,

It's no wonder

They were running out of time

She only wondered

what took them so long to admit:

"We're all madly in love here"

The Myths

Time

is always mad crazy

always crazy mad timing

Always changing the tides

Constantly missing each other

Waving goodbye

Consistently evolving

Constantly

both too afraid of shorelines

To meet each other halfway

Loving each other halfway

Settling for friendship

That never crashed against the shoreline of

Rocky possibilities for a romantic relationship

Both too caught up

By half moon phases

To pull each other in

Kept pulling away instead

Like the ocean searching for sandcastles To

romanticize about

& shower with love from afar

Desire at a distance

But not too distant

Their full moon dreaming thus far

Too caught up

To fall

in love

Their restless hearts

Resisting gravity

Like Cupid resisting Chronos

It's no wonder the god of time

Would want to clip the wings of

an irresponsible

love baby.

Baby, Love

Feels irresponsible

with him

because God is timing them

Clipping down their last lap around this

track Tracking them

While they...

are running out of time

The Turning Tables

Again and again running in circles

Like the earth & the sun

Endlessly circling each other

But never quite in orbit

Like an endless game of checkers:

Where he moves she moves

But they only get one move

So naturally...

When he finally made his move

. . she moved

But he were never one to follow

She waited for him

Even waited on him

But the tables she was serving

Were never meant for turning

Meanwhile he was always turning tables

Patiently waiting his turn

He turned the records over

But they never set the record straight

For the record

He played their records

Always on cue

She'll never forget

that playlist he made for them

"From me to you"

A modern day mixtape

She'll not forget

And prays he too will 'forget-me-not'

She'll always remember him as

Her hometown love

Her schoolgirl crush

Her oldest friend

She will not forget

The day she knew

He loved her too

For Insecure Girls

To all the girls with their heads in the clouds
And bare feet barely planted on the ground
Who know gut feelings are guardian angels
And think

To the girls with the body image issues
Beautiful girls,
Girls like me,
Who don't always feel beautiful
Who question their beauty
Wonder about their worth
And don't always know
What everyone else seems to know
To the girls with insecurities a mile high
And self esteem lower than the tides
To the girls who are not so sure

For the girls in need of body confidence
Better beauty politics
For the females getting in formation
With the Natural hair movement
the Black is beautiful movement
And the fat acceptance movement

Making efforts to decolonize beauty routines
Reclaiming agency
Reinforcing self-love ethics
And teaching our own minds what to think of
and consider as:
beautiful, brilliant, gorgeous, talented, fabulous, & powerful
beyond measure
Who have thrown away crowns for a type of people
pleasing unfit for a queen

Who have thrown away every unruly ruler, tape measure,
or measuring cup

that has ever presumed to contain an artificial ounce of a woman's worth
Trading self-worth for the approval of men instead of training our hearts to know the
theology of a goddess
Of a virtuous ruby
Or a hidden proverb
The value of a gem
Or a sanctuary
more precious
More virtuous
Than a man's hands could know what to do with

For the girls who have spent more time counting calories than counting blessings
Who forgot to kiss their bodies every morning
After awakening each day to still find themselves living in a daydream
Embodying that dream
A dreamboat of a body
A cathedral for a flesh
An image of a God
So perfect we cannot dare to look the Son directly in the eye
It's no wonder we do not know the value of a woman
Or understand our own self worth

Instead we let lovers who have never been taught to love or ever been trained to fly
fly too close to our Sun
and when they fall because the glory of a goddess is too much for a mere mortal
We never blame the boy who reached too high for a star too brilliant
Too out of his reach
We blame the sun, that is also a star, for being too much
Too bright
Too beautiful
Too fire on high
Or not enough

Not enough warmth
Or enough soft glow
Not enough to let a man living on a prayer
Cast his shadow wishes in the lightness of her being

For the sunshine girls with sunflower hearts
And shadows that cast an iridescent glow
Who have convinced themselves
Or let ourselves be convinced
That we are too much and not enough
This is how we lose ourselves

For these girls
Girls like me, who forget their worth as easily as we forget the ones who "loved" us
Sunshine girls with sunset hearts
For the sacred ones
The Forgetful ones
Who work twice as hard to forgive themselves
And remind ourselves we are angles in the making

We are the girls with the five year plans
With the diet plans
The meal plans
The fitness routine
And the meditation regimens

We are the girls with all the questions
And not enough answers
The girls with too many daydreams
And not enough vision boards

We are the girls who never learned to love ourselves
All this education and they never taught us how to

We are the girls with a complicated list of past lovers
The rebel fighters
The girls with the sugar cravings
And the broken dream catchers

We are the girls who stay up late
And get the munchies
The girls with curves
And not enough language
For positive self talk

We are the girls running out of vocabulary
And running out of time for boys
And patience for men who are not worth our time
We are the women reclaiming language

For fighter girls
And well read women
Girls who know more than one language
And understand deep metaphors hidden
within the wells of a well written poem

For poetic girls
Girls like me
Who have cried themselves to sleep
But are finally awakening

We are the ones we have all been waiting for
Awake o dreamer…

                                        Beware of the risen ones.

Anything And Absolutely Everything

What does it mean to be human when empathy and strength are not mutually exclusive?

What does it mean to be human?
Is it to be resilient?
To need food?
To know hunger?
To have experienced exhaustion
Or to seek out rest?
Is it our desperate desire for love
Or lust
That makes us human?

What does it mean to be human?
To have zero impulse control
And feel powerless?
Or to have so much power
That we feel fully in control?

What does it mean to be human?
To know suffering
Or embody resilience?
Is it our uncanny ability to hold it all together
When we are clearly falling apart?
Is it bloodlines?
Or emotions?
Or the insurmountable ability
To feel
Anything
At any moment?
Is it our capacity for love that makes us human?
Or that we are made of star stuff
With beating hearts
Made for love yet powerless against death itself?

What is it?
This thing that makes us human?

Is it our sensation for pain?
Or our tolerance for trauma?
The humiliation of utter human agony
Or our ability to understand the suffering of one another
In a way that is almost divine?

What is this that makes us human?
But empathy itself
The singular most empowering thing
Any human could ever do for another:

To be *strong* for someone
While also *suffering* alongside them

To know weakness
and glory
simultaneously
Through feel-it-all-human-sincerity

This is the most human form of anything
and absolutely everything
that still exists under the sun.

For The Ones With The Bulletproof Chests

If love is truly
a battle field
then most people
are war vets.

I've heard legends about
warrior lovers with
amputated hearts
that turned their vests
into bullet proof chests
No longer differentiating
enemies from allies
love from war
or white flags from battle cries
all because their hearts have all turned to purple.

For most, it's not the war that we regret,
But the PTSD it left us with.
The very entity that stands in our own way
of letting us love you
or letting us
be loved in return

Fluent

We're not really strangers

We are lovers passing by

Speaking two different languages

Attempting to decode the way we feel

With glances

And unintentional ... intentional touches

That say more

Than any language ever could

We analyze one another

Spanish

English

It would not matter

You are the letter to my body

That our ancestors wrote

I watch the way you move

Loving every mannerism

It's as though,

Whatever your body language is,

I am certain

I speak it.

Two Sides, Same Coin

On my best days I am
everything they told me not to be
Gaslit revolution
Set aflame by their fuel
Call me crazy
I am a jungle thing
My ancestor's wildest dreams

On my worst days
I am everything they taught me not to be
Dimly lit candle light
In the corner of a room
No one enters through
Self-illuminating
Warming no one
other than myself
My ancestor's most dreadful nightmare
Only worse

On my best days
I belong to the people
                  to the cause
                        the collective
                & the garden of our God

But on my worst days
I belong only to myself
                      I am isolated
                      all alone
                      a mere placeholder of a frame
              barely bearing the image of a God
        we've all lost sight of

Unrecognizable
Even to myself

but most days…

Fire, flame, or flicker
I am
eternal wick
set ablaze
in the burrows
of my bones
Can't shut up
Won't sit still
Burning bush
Consuming
Driest bones
with heaven's rain
I'm speaking to it
Bringing back to life
I am
Resurrected girl
I am
Phoenix girl
Rising
Rising
Restored from ashes
& shadow valleys
bursting through
beneath unbreakable body
receiving power
with a growing glow
& a tongue of fire

overcoming the
tradition of silence
in the land of the living
set on fire
female fire.

re·cur·ring

/rəˈkəriNG/

adjective
a dream experienced repeatedly over time

The Writer & Sweet Body

Sometimes I cannot choose
Between the writer and the body

Both parts of me
Demand my time
My attention
Forcing their way into the pilot seat
Hoping to be the one calling the shots

Most times I find it impossible to choose
both Body and the writer

So I choose one over the other
Sacrificing the latter in order to preserve the chosen one
Whichever one she gets to be today

When I choose the body over Writer
Body is content,
She is filled to the brim
She not only sleeps, she rests
She is invigorated and feels fully alive
Each breath Body takes becomes a reminder
of both her strength and her capabilities
She moves muscles until they ache
and allows for their recovery
She takes in the earth and becomes one with the world around her.
She is well fed
She eats clean
She indulges in the pleasures that taste and scent allot her.
She bathes in the aroma of bath salts and bath bombs
She even writes with mere delight,
Taking pleasure in her friend: the writer.

When I choose the body over Writer,
Body is grateful,
She is well taken care of and is much better
at sharing space
I remind Body much more often why and how much
I truly cherish her and
I express my committed
To Body's affirmation and well being.

But when I chose Writer over the body
Everything is neglected
Especially sweet Body.
Writer she is vicious and unrelenting
She takes and takes and hardly knows how to give back
except for words.
Writer is great at giving us her word,
But never anything more.
Like Body Writer is also beautiful, but her beauty and
the sustainability of her lifestyle
come at such high cost
Which Body pays a daily price for each minute that
Writer pilots
When Writer is in control of our creative freedom it's as
if she holds Body hostage
until the work is done.
Writer is brilliant the way she builds monuments out of
metaphors and creates cathedrals
from mere imagination
But Writer is selfish, not always, but she can be
self-indulgent and unaware which mixes as a terrible
cocktail she then forces Body to drink
straight no chaser
There is no chasing Writer down when she is in
production mode.
She forces Body back into slavery and takes away more
Than she could ever repay her

Body is keeping the score
Holding every trauma in tension
Head, shoulders, knees, and toes,
While Writer calls the shots
One after another
Writer pushes Body so hard
she almost dives off the deep end

And for what?
For a few well written poems,
well crafted soliloquies,
and some intricate use of word play?
But all work and no play makes Body a dull girl
Writer can be laser focused, not always, though when she is
She is unforgiving
To herself
To Body
To myself
Yet we drive each other straight into the ground
No brakes.

Whenever I choose Body over Writer
Body becomes a gift to us both that only knows how to give back in multiplied measures

But if ever I choose Writer over Body
Writer struggles to share the spotlight and I forget
that she is a soloist and that I am responsible
for never teaching Writer how to play well with others

Poor Body, used neglected Body,
Tries to advocate for herself
Begs me to sustain her
To hold space for her
To let her feel

To feed her
To give her rest
But I don't
Body aches and groans and yawns
begging us for our attention
For consistency, for love
But we don't give in
We do not check in or scan Body
To ask her "Where does it hurt?"
Instead we silence and ignore her
because Writer is producing
She is performing and creating.
And we've convinced ourselves: *she must*.

Or worse, we've been convinced: *she must not stop.*

Who says no to Writer?
She is the most charming and convincing sweet talker
So when she says, "Everything is fine,"
You believe her

Even if it means that Body
is back there
somewhere
Aching
Dying
Raising her voice and
Shouting at the top of her lungs: "EVERYTHING HURTS!"

Sweet Body, barely still alive, is praying to be felt
Desperately needing to be seen and acknowledged,
but we can't hear her
Let alone feel her
Our foots' fallen asleep
Everything part of Body has gone numb (smell / taste)

Because when Writer says, "Everything's fine,"
We want
and need
so desperately
to believe her.

My Vulnerability

Lives Somewhere Between

Every Temptation To Keep My Guard Up

And The Ever Complex Attempt

To Leave My Heart Wide Open

I Grew Up Barefoot

I grew up barefoot

Now I didn't say I grew up poor

I said I grew up barefoot

Running towards the Son

Kneeling in the dirt of my great grandfathers' land.

A holy land

Milk & honey

Before greed & money

Knee deep in the soil that that inspired

barefeet people and bareback writers

I grew up barefoot

Chasing sheep

And counting cattle in the land of Mayan ancestors

Racing wild horses

With our hearts racing wild

In a land that gave us everything

I never wanted anything

I grew up barefoot

Running towards my sisters

Curls to the wind

Dancing to the songs of the city
La bachatera, as we called it,
The music of our soul and
Our soul, la anción de la colonia

Toes tickled by Caribbean heat
As we slept smushed together in a bed we outgrew
I watched my sisters braid each other's hair
I listened as mami sang the Spanish lullaby: "Arroz con leche"
Smelled the scent of wet soil sneak in with the breeze
Until we'd fall asleep and wake up the next morning to an unforgiving Latin sun
Beating against our brown skin and bare feet

I grew up barefoot
Now I didn't say I grew up poor
I said I grew up free

Rearview Mirror

I hope my greatest moments are ahead of me

I pray I did not leave something of value in the rearview mirror.

Transported

Every now and then my mom will say a word or phrase that transports me back to a time before my time. Reminding me that she was once a Honduran girl before she was a mother, a wife, an American woman. Reminding me how she had a whole life, was an entire person before she became the woman I now know her to be. She was a holistic individual I never even met. A human I know almost nothing about. As she existed in this alternative life before I arrived, during her time before my time. She spoke sayings, used idioms, and bantered about things I wouldn't understand, with loved ones I will never meet. These days I know her as a woman, mother, wife, and strong female. I never knew her as a young girl, small child, scared adolescent seeking protection. Sometimes Mami says a phrase and I'm reminded how little I know of her. And how much she was before I came along. How there once was a time in our space and time continuum where she was so much more than the little I know. Through one simple word of hers I am transported. It just takes one simple Spanish expression and she reminds me ..as I am reminded, of the fullness of her. Where she comes from. Who she was. What she's learned. The mistakes and lessons that make her. The people she's known and the friends who have endlessly loved her back. "Yo también soy de mis machetes," my mother exclaims as she throws her head back with a child-like laughter and all at once I understand she is made up of more memory than I can hold. She is magic. Like me, she is who she is, because of where she's from and the people that raised her.

No Way To Love
sometimes we are so guarded we cannot feel a thing

I love you
The way the ground loves a snowflake
Quickly
And desperately
and yet never for long enough

Feelings dissipating before contact is made
I can't quite hold you
& you don't quite capture me

Everything fading before
Anything comes into focus
Like a polaroid in reverse

I love you in the way a snowflake loves the
ground So much, yet not enough
With every molecular ounce of my being
Melting into you until
Even Whoville is lost to us
And we can't tell who's who
Because we've merged being with identity
And our identities have fused together

I love you the way frozen precipitation
loves the warm soil of the earth
With not enough time.
Every moment of affection
A stolen moment of someone else's time

Sadly, this is no way to love another soul.

By The Time it Reached Her

The last time

He saw her

She was crying

He whispered in her ear

Something sweet about forever

and it sounded kind of special,

but by the time it reached her

she heard it as "goodbye."

How does one respond when "I love you"

is used synonymously with goodbye?

Comparing Thee To A Summer's Day

He felt like a day off from work,
But not just any day off
He was a Ferris Bueller day off
or a vacation day with accrued paid time off.

He was like the first day of school
equal parts terrifying and thrilling.

He was that feeling of
coasting downhill on a
bicycle during a late night sunset ride.

He was the feeling of self-discovery
Like solving a Rubik's cube
Or tasting your favorite dessert for the first time
He was a home cooked meal
A tiny piece of home
Like a constellation that follows you around in the sky
To every country you've ever traveled to

He was
peppermint tea in the morning
And comfort food in the evening

Like celery juice
That you just know is good for you
He became her nutritional value for everything.

Calling It Even

They both

Said "I love you"

They just meant different things.

She meant, she'd give up anything for him

While he meant, he'd give her up for anything.

Neither understood what the other meant,

So they just chose to call it even.

Unlike me, yet like me

Beautiful girl on the street intersection

Of Seward Highway and Fireweed Lane

You are about my age

I looked you in the eyes

We've never met

Yet we are not strangers

What is your story?

Where do you come from?

How did we find ourselves here:

With you, standing on the corner of this busy

intersection

as I press whatever change I have left into the palm

of your hands?

we are the same age.

Theoretically

She was a metaphor

He was a math equation

Never on the same page,

They couldn't quite add up

Their love was the one problem neither could solve,

which made for a love that lived only in theory.

Cardiomyopathy

If a girl's heart breaks

and no one is around to heal it

does it really bleed?

Cardiac Arrest

If a boy's heart breaks

and no one is around to stop the

bleeding, or hold pressure,

or do compressions,

does he ever heal?

Silent Prayers

On the days he thinks of her

He seldom reaches out

He simply whispers to himself:

"I hope today she doesn't doubt herself"

Some Truths & A Lie

I am steam, fire, engine, and train itself
I am brass knuckles and big mistakes
Huge identity and no missed takes

I am hurricane and ocean water
Tsunami with no boundary
Girl with no border
No home
No land
Yet, I am no man's land

Nomad
In pastures that offer little rest and hearts that ache

I am belly full of laughs and eyes full of tears but she is not

She is the land I inhabit
with peace of mind and quiet
while I am all thrill, she is stillness and sunrise
while I am nightfall, she is ember,
And with midnight magic I embody all things
she cannot become

She is translucent
Empty and giant like a black hole
Full of herself
She is apathetic and indifferent
Clueless she becomes trapped by her own force
Of spaceless wander and a starry war she's created
She may be knight,
but I am jedi
I am force to be reckoned with
She is less envy, just acceptance;

just accept me
contentment at its best
She is endlessly forgiving;
She is passivity and hope
Lightweight and
gentle tempest
While I am raging sea
She is the clam in me
While I am both she somehow makes me neither
She sits in me like a crumb at the pit of my bottomless belly
Somewhere deep within me where I can tap into her
Engage all that she is if I just reach deep enough to digest all the worst parts of me

Or maybe I am hers?...
But if I am in her...
I rage within her like butterfly in the pit of her stomach
I do not go gentle
I do not go quiet
I do not go into the night without a fight
for if she is gentle, I am giant

But she is all the opposite
Reclaiming language
She is all the rave
Everything I'm not
She is firefly light waiting to be caught
She is theirs
Freely her best
Coiled somewhere in between their hands

Gasping
Trying
Fighting
To stay alive.

Skeletal

Everything is unfinished.

Her story has yet to be fleshed out,

But even as you see her now

Existing here before you

This woman in her skeletal form

Haunts his memories,

His sleepless nights,

And brings him chills down through his spine

For even in her hollowness

She is brick-house made of bones.

subletting rent free in the closet of his home

Atomic

She didn't know about love bombing

until he Hiroshima'd her heart

and called it an act of love.

Rock Bottom

When they first met, her heart sank.

Since then,
She's turned herself into an anchor
And learned to swim.
Taught herself
to breath under water,
and know the feeling of lungs on fire,
so she no longer holds her breath for him.

When they first met, her heart sank

Since then,
She perfected the art of soul alchemy
and transformed herself from
metal weapon of self-defense
Into guardian for her heart of gold

When they first met, her heart sank

He was playing battleship with her heart
Calling it love and all along
She never even knew they were at war

For Heart-Sleeved Humans

it's easy to fall in love with poets:

Dreamers who have mastered

the art of soul-spilling,

word-bending romantics

wearing inky

hearts on fingertips

Loving better on paper

Than we do on people

Leaving behind beauty marks

on the hearts on which we choose to imprint

and the souls we seek to love on paper.

Crying Over Spilled Tea

Last week I spilled honey on my keyboard while making tea

Ever since, it's taken a little more work to type the letter "K"

Words like "knickknack" have become a hassle

And now the letter "O"

Which sits right above k

has also given up

Both letters refusing to show up

No matter how hard I push or press

it's becoming more and more difficult

to write the words

"I am o.k."

Heart Condition

I was born with a small hole in my heart

They called it a murmur

Occasionally it whispers to me

in the form of an abnormal heart rhythm

My heart literally skips beats

on a regular basis

So it's no wonder

I've been unable to decipher my feelings for you

Ever since we met

Because my heart's been playing tricks on me

Ever since I was born

The hole has since been closed

But I am still unsure if it was you

or something else

that filled it.

25th Hour

If there were a twenty-fifth hour in the day,

I'd probably spend it with you

Or I'd spend the hour

with poetry

Well, truthfully,

if I had a twenty-fifth hour in my day

I would probably spend it

writing poetry about you.

She fell for him so hard, she almost didn't realize
the fall had left a scar.

The Turning Page

He became the cave Plato wrote about,

The inferno Dante dreamt of,

And the muses who personified pain.

She wondered if he knew it wasn't a compliment

To have hurt another human so deeply

To have inspired countless allegories about love

and loss

But as she turned the page

which immortalized their love

She turned him into art

With every verse & rhyme.

Honestly

He spoke in hypotheticals.

She loved him in metaphors.

When life asked them to speak honestly

They inevitably got lost in translation.

Out of the blue

She walks at a pace

About six feet in front of me

It is still winter

But spring has sprung

We walk in puddles and slush

Her feet leaving prints behind her

They feel as though they are meant for me

Being left for me

Naturally,

I try my best

With every footstep

To step where she has stepped

And left a mark for me

Secretly I'm hoping to discover

What it might feel like

To walk a mile in her shoes

To sense,

However briefly,

What it must feel like

To be her.

Is there truly such a thing as falling in love in a matter of minutes?

What

is

on

the

other

side

of

pain?

Poetry.

Mad Hatter

She fell in love with his charm,

with the sort of way he poured the world for her

into little cups of coffee filled with wonder

But in the end it was his madness that broke her heart

and pushed her further and further away

Into subterranean obscurity

Into the deepest parts of someone else's rabbit hole.

Eye of the Storm

I'll admit,

Sometimes I am both the wind and the sails

The push and the pull

The turbulence itself

while you find ways to become the anchor

That tethers me to the earth.

Keeping me afloat

You do your absolute best

To save me from myself.

I Don't Always Say "I love you"

Sometimes I say:
Buckle up
I'm sorry
Did you get your brakes checked
Want me to make you your favorite snack
Did you eat enough today
Would you like some tea
How was your day
Did you have a good lunch
How do you feel
Are you sure you're getting enough sleep
Be safe
Please text me when you get there
Are you okay
I'm proud of you
If you need anything I'm here
I'll sleep with my phone on loud
Want to share my umbrella
Don't forget your keys
Thank you for yesterday
Some days I'll just send flowers
Or leave a note
Or let you sleep in
Or laugh at your jokes
Or take you on one of those long drives you like
We can even pass that lake you love
While we listen to your favorite album
Or whichever one you're in the mood for today

I don't always say "I love you,"
Sometimes I just
Squeeze your hand
Find ways to remind you I'm glad you're here
Ask to cuddle after a long fight

Call you pet names during a fight
Call you back after you've hung up
Hold back all my judgments
Hold space for all your tears
And sit with you until the wave passes
Reach over to stroke the back of your head while you drive
Kiss your cheek while you do something mundane
Just... stare at you..
Let you pick the restaurant
Ask you what you need
Stay up late and watch anime with you
Laugh so hard until both our stomachs hurt
Ask you what you want
...insist until you tell me
Let you be vulnerable
And do the work to understand you
Go on "adventures" with you which is sometimes just 2am runs to a drive-thru for some midnight milkshakes Sometimes I just write you a poem ...like this one
Or let you ruin book endings for me
Because I know that I'll forgive you
Sometimes I just forgive you
Or I learn your taste in music
Proof read your poetry and give you specific feedback because I know you like that
Send scriptures that remind me of you
Give you compliments that are oddly specific
And I always let you have the last slice of dessert
Most importantly,   I
never
ever
leave
you.

I don't always say "I love you"
I just do my best to *stay*
And care
And continue to choose you over leaving.

When I stay I show you I love you
by reminding you how your best
is more than enough...

Honestly,
I hope you know,
I don't always *say* "I love you"
Because I have found a million other ways
to relay the same sentiment
and let you *feel* my love.

Touring Musician

He held her the way a musician holds his guitar,
but in his hands she didn't feel instrumental.

She felt more like an object
Fully aware of his lack of objectivity
She grew consequently aware of how
he turned her body into object
For his amusement
A muse
For him to play with
And temporarily perform with
Like a touring musician
He held her the only way that he knew how to:
At arms length
With calluses on his fingertips
And one hand on the chord
Ready to pull the plug
Ending their tour early
he played her without encore.

Dear Educated Girl,

Do not dumb yourself down. It's okay to be the most __fill-in-the-blank__ girl in the room. Don't let their insecurities eclipse who you are. Find your voice and claim it. Know your points and state them. Never let the good, the toxic, or the masculine make you feel as though there is not a space for you or your voice because let me tell you. Abuela worked too hard to break open spaces for us and mami didn't raise no fool. You are the daughter of Eve, I wish you'd let yourself have your "serpent's tongue and overcome the tradition of silence." Keep reading keep writing, but integrate voices that sound like yours too because it may not be included in the curriculum. Read Julia Alvares, Sandra Cisneros, Junot Diaz, Richard Rodriguez, Paulo Coelho. Find poets like Elizabeth Acevedo and Denice Frohman who write about accents and Afro-Latinidad. Read them and know them. Learn to recognize the sound of your voice before and after translation.

Yours truly

Treasure Map

It was the way he was looking at her that night

That made her feel such foreign feelings

Like a tourist to her own beauty

She couldn't imagine what he was seeing

Face to face for the first time

What she had only glimpsed from time to time

in her own reflection

He gazed at her with such inquiry

Like a conquistador wanting to discover more

Already envious of every exquisite thing about her

He tried to wade into her waters

Which kept her lost as see

Until she asked him for a roadmap

And he drew a picture of his love instead

Here he had found his treasure

Hidden somewhere in her heart

And he knew as he looked at her

X had marked the spot.

Isn't It Funny

How people become our context for everything
Our vantage point for beauty, for heartache,
and every familiar feeling in-between.

Isn't it funny,
How people seamlessly shape-shift into our lives and
become a point of reference for every experience.
Suddenly every memory
Good or bad
Every lesson
moral or evil
is eternally tethered to another human life
Tied to the memory of a person we once
Loved,
Admired,
Despised,
Or envied

Isn't it beautiful,
All the little things we didn't know we didn't know
until someone taught us
All the feelings we never felt before
until someone provoked us
Or in some cases inspired us

Isn't it hysterical
How afterwards,
we can't seem to forget these human beings
Who so eloquently strung themselves together
Like sentences at the end of our life long paragraphs

Isn't it humorous
How easily our lives are intertwined
Yet it's a game of Russian roulette

for the ones we remember and the ones we forget

Isn't it funny,
But mostly
not funny at all,
How some people imprint on us
Like triggers being pulled inside our memory bank
Manipulating moments
Past, present, future tense
Like bullies with bullets
Triggering the exquisite,
along with gut-wrenching agony
and everything in-between

Isn't it not funny at all,
How often with or without our choice
People become personified gunfire
After our memories betray us and
Provide them with the gunpowder?

Groceries
written after the stranger in passing shouted the racist slurs and I was asked if I did anything to provoke him ……. also written after countless interactions throughout my day.

The truth is,
sometimes when people look at me
or do a quick double take
and break their neck
following me around with the eyes
at a grocery store
at a bank
in the park
during a poetry reading
at a checkout line
on a plane
in the airport
in a tree
on a train
in a box
with a fox
I hardly ever know if it's because they think I'm beautiful or a threat
Is it because they've never seen someone who looks like me
or is it the way I wrapped my hair that day
or both?
Is it the color of my skin
or the fact that I didn't wrap my fro that day
or both?
Is it my melanin that shocks them
or my beauty that throws them
or my curls that stun and surprise them
or is it all of the above?
Are they amazed
or appalled?

What circus freak am I being forced to play today?
What circus act can I perform for you?
Would it be enough to just be brown in America
Or is that too much entertainment for one day?
The opposite of family friendly,
not really what the viewers want.
Tell me, please, what is expected of me?
Am I wild creature?
Exotic Amazonian in her natural habitat?
Or am I simply brown body,
terror-like-hair wrapped into a threat
standing in your way?
What am I supposed to be today?
Most days I cannot tell.

The truth is,
sometimes when people look at me
or do a quick double take
and break their neck
following me around with the eyes
I hardly ever know
if it is because I am beautiful or brown
in the best or worst case possible
in the eyes of my beholder
I hardly ever know if I should feel flattered or afraid,
but I'll tell you one thing:
rarely do I feel safe.

When I walk into a store on 60th and Burnside
and they stare
I am fully aware of all the white gazes that have noticed me
and while I shop the furthest thing from my mind is my grocery list about bananas and
avocado and plant based products
because the first thing on my mind

is the last thing on all of theirs.
While I shop I ask myself:
Will I make it down this aisle?
Will I make it to the checkout line?
Will I make it to my car?
and all the way back home?
Will I make it safely?
Will I be safe then?
Instead of asking myself:
Did I grab enough sofrito and canela?
I ask myself why the man is still staring?
Yet as he does this,
I am the one glancing around for allies and emergency exit routes,
counting all the doors and searching for people that look like me.
I have forgotten bread more than once
I have cut my grocery list in half more than once
I have tried to leave the store quicker more than once
All because their eyes were watching me
and I couldn't quite tell if it was because of beauty or melanin;
Mere admiration or subtle hatred convoluted in a stranger's glance.
Nevertheless, it is in these moments that I do not feel seen
I only feel watched.

So I do my best to remove myself from their line of sight
And I do not stand in anybody's way,
Regardless of beauty or brownness
I wish only to be invisible
From the ones who stare.

Some have the courage to say something
Which isn't always courage

Sometimes just an an excuse or explanation to justify the staring

I wonder if they think it's rude or a compliment
I wonder if they care how I receive it

Some are bold enough to say:
"I like your hair!"
"I love your wrap!"
"You are so beautiful!"

While others are just bold enough to yell out crude remarks and call me ugly names
Which, they don't realize, only makes them hideous

But most?
Most are only bold enough to stare.

Brown Girls In America Ask:

Mirror Mirror on the wall,

Is *white* still fairest of them all?

Dreamboat Means Translating Streams of Consciousness

My entire life has been comprised of switching codes
And moving between modes
                          of being
Thinking in two languages
Listening to Mami and Papi speak to me in Spanish
While I respond in English

I try my best to speak in one language
But for the most part
        I think and dream in Spanglish
              Write poetry in Spanglish
                      Remember memories in Spanglish

Separating the two languages has often felt
        more violent than harmonious;
              somehow hijacking who I am supposed to be;

a more silent, subtle form of murder

I'm often trying to find the right words in English, but always find them quicker in Spanish
Most of the day's energy is spent
translating my own thoughts
So others are not lost in translation

But for this sequence of poetry I will not edit
language Or derail my bi-lingual train of thought

Instead, I invite you to experience my poetry with as much duality as I create it
And partake in these pieces

With me
As I write with a psyche that is no longer split
And reveal a realized dream that is no longer interrupted.

rest·less·ness

/ˈres(t)ləsnəs/

noun
the inability to rest or relax; insomnia

Last

Night

I

Could

Not

Sleep,

So

I

Stayed

Awake

To

Dream

Pillow Fight

She told herself

Not to lose herself

Though most days

For him, she was willing to get lost

But by nightfall

She was searching all her dreams For

pieces of herself

She must have left buried somewhere

deep within his nightmares

While wrestling sleep

she scratched at her pillow cases

which could not fight her back.

Body Language

The first time
You held me in your arms
My body noticed
How you asked it
For permission

You draped your arms around me
Like a question mark
And every move of your hand
Became a comma or a semicolon
Pausing to second guess itself

Every movement of your body
slow, timid, and anxious
Like the awkwardness of a middle school boy
Raising his hand in the back of his class
Silently begging for attention
Waiting, patiently, to turn his quiet into a question

                        As if that were enough

The second time
you held me in your arms
Your body still a stutter
Struggling to tell me what it wanted
But after repeated attempts you found a way
To ask the question
Reaching for me from across the pier
You placed your hand behind my shoulder
As if simply to remind me that you were still there

                        And it was enough

The next time
You held me

In your arms
It was poetry.

The last time
You held me
I was praying
it wouldn't be
the last

That time
You cradled me in your arms
Like an outdated cliché
And I cried this time
But you married our hands together like a metaphor
And tucked me tighter into the nook of your neck
And arms
Mortar, brick, and martyr
You built yourself into a bridge for me
I didn't know it at the time
But you would help me to transition

The last time
you held me
In your arms
You wove your body into a nest for me
Made something out of nothing for me
And cradled every part of me
The way a cocoon cradles a caterpillar
For the last time, its sole purpose being to let it go

I hadn't noticed until then
How every time you held me
You were getting ready to let go.

Some

lovers

have

nothing

more

to

offer

than

triggers

for

your

trauma

Another word

When he becomes the dream you cannot wake up from,

know that another word for this is *night terror*.

What if I want to be more

than a dream within your dream?

Restraining Order

Last night another man died
His skin the same color as my own
His hair the same texture as mine

This morning I woke up
With a pain in my chest
As my body fought to file a restraining order against life itself
Showing me how it carried the pain of a thousand generations
How it held the weight of tired men and restless women on its shoulders.

This morning I woke up
With a pain in my chest
As my body bore witness without shame
For the countless burdens that buried themselves in the skin of black and brown bodies

Last night another man died
His skin the same color as mine
His hair the same texture as my own

This morning my heart woke up in a crooked knot
Distressed by the fact that I could read the first lines of this poem on any day of the week

and this statement could still hold to be true.

Having People And Not Having People

When she wakes at 2:30am

sobbing and unable to catch her breath

She wonders who she can call

She's been working so hard

She wonders if they will still recognize her

When her heart is aching she wonders

Who will be around to hold her

When she wakes at 2:30am

sobbing and unable to catch her breath

She asks herself:

"What did I bury?" and

"Where have I buried it?"

I

knew

it

was

love

because

it

required

my

whole

being.

Deal

She plays it safe.

He makes her want to go all in.
But she plays it safe.

He doesn't.
He reads her cards like an open letter
Sees right through her poker face

She plays it safer.

He gambles

A lot.

Makes her want to fold.

But then he looks at her.
In that way that only he can see her
And she looks back
Barely
Only for a second
Because she talks with her eyes
And he reads her like a deck of cards
But mainly because
she plays it safe

But there in his altruistic eyes
She can tell:
He isn't bluffing
& he's not a cheater.

They've both just lost
So much
in the past
Being forced to fold
After going all in

The cost is high now so they protect what's left
Both playing the game a little differently now

But playing together
Has raised the stakes

He looks at her: "it's your move"
She looks at him
And he's certainly lost
Here's how they won
Both playing the game
By showing their cards.

For Fighters Who Are Also Lovers

For the adults who never got to be children
For the ones who put their armor on too quickly
Even when it didn't fit
8 sizes too big
For the tiny humans who faced giants far too early
For the children who were told they couldn't be children
And instead became soldiers
For the one who are dearly loved but were poorly loved
For the ones who became poets and advocates
Still making up for all the words never said
and the worlds that they missed out on.
For the lovers who were forced to fight too early
And the fighters who became lovers
In spite of the fight
& despite the fact
That every instinct had been re-wired...
For those lovers still loving
with a fight and fire beneath their belly
keeping us all warm
though we will never understand . .
For those ones
You immortal humans
The greatest lovers of all time:
We see you
Still need you
and we are so, so sorry.

Howl

He turned the butterfly nest in the pit of her stomach into a

beehive

His love, painful to her touch

Like a sting that almost killed them both

Her heart, still swollen from the pain he left her with.

How it stung when he said he loved her

While holding another

Knowing full well he still loved another

It was unfair

The way he eclipsed her

This boy crying wolf

The way he howled for her

Howled at a deaf moon

Night after night

Only to keep her up

His "I love yous" materializing like monsters

Underneath her bed.

Whisper

He was the wishing well

That never made any of her dreams come true.

When her change hit rock bottom

the only sound that ricocheted back

Was an echo

A delirious dream she tossed into his emptiness

In the form of a prayer

But blasphemy was all he ever gave her

Empty promises

Unfulfilled wishes

Unrealized dreams

He became the echo that could only mirror

The appearance of affection

And what was left of love

A resounding noise

Impossible to decipher

A long distance call mumbling something about I'm sorry

A call she would not return

His echo quieted by her vacant whisper

Echo

When he says "I love you too"
Remember he is just an echo
mimicking the sound of your own affection
There is no return on investment here
He cannot love you back
He will try, but
He will not know how to
He is only Echo
He may even want to
But this is just poor loverboy's attempt
To give you riches he's not good for
without a dollar to his name
He's still indebted to the last girl that broke his heart
When their commitment was foreclosed on
He's still making good on those broken promises
Paying his forgiveness to her in installments
sweet sister, this is not love
It is a gamble
Requiring a down pain-ment you cannot bank on
Your feelings you will loan him
But you cannot afford to lose

Echo does not know love
He is your own desire bouncing back at you
Fabrications of your own imagination and whatever you wish to hear
Your mind filling in blanks for what you wish to see
After all the change you invested in his wishing well
This is your own desire gone mad.

Maddening as it is,
sweet girl, this is not love

Though he sounds a lot like it
Repetition after repetition,
When he finally reaches you
He will no longer be love
He is Echo.
                              Learn to hear the difference.

Anchor

They say: "the most challenging relationship

is the healthy one after the toxic one"

I don't know if they're right

Or if I believe they are wrong

What I do know is:

    Ever since I met you

        I can't quite catch my breath

            Thing is,

        I cannot tell whether it is

    We are drowning

    or coming up for air.

We enter this world
crying,   kicking,   screaming,
and covered in someone else's blood.

This should not be the way we also leave this life

Shadow

She had such a profound capacity for pain.

When she realized she had the capacity

to hold his shadow by her side

She knew her first mistake

Was making friends with

the monsters in his head,

the skeletons in his closet,

and she never should have spoken

to the snakes living in his garden.

Accents

If love ends in a foreign language

and no one is around to translate

is it truly lost?

What if we can't fall back asleep?

What if all this time…

the dream we've been trying to recover

is the dream we never should've dreamt?

Interrupted Sleep Patterns

When a poem wakes you up in the middle of the night

Begging to be written down

Begging to be heard

You listen

You write it down

and someday,

You read that one out aloud.

Love and Civility

When she can no longer hold him in her arms

She will hold him in her memory

Exactly as he is:

Brilliant and beautiful,

sensitive soul,

Poetry reading,

Porter drinking,

Brown skin boy with the hazelnut coffee eyes

& the Cory Mathews hair

She will remember him as bulletproof

Except on their date nights

when he left his guard at home

And extended out a peaceful drawbridge for her

to climb under

And surrender into

With all her baggage

filled to the brim with white flags

She materialized as a peace treaty

Which he treated with his peace

His love and civility.

Aerial Somersaults

He will immortalize her in his memory

Memorialize their time together

Exactly as it was:

These feelings he will not forget

Brown and yellow purple blue

He will hold her in suspension

the way a trapeze artist

Holds themself up

Over a celestial balance beam

In tension

He'll suspend these memories in his head

Hold moments as hostages in his mind

In an attempt to freeze time

All this

So he never has to learn

what happens

When a heart lets go.

The Acrobat

She'll perform aerial apparatuses with her thoughts of him

Try not to romanticize what might have been

What could have been

What they always wanted

And almost had

Before the spinning, the swinging, the flying through the air

Fell flat

The room before them,

A deafening silence.

Did he have any idea, a trapeze act can be performed solo?

Departure Gate

She wanted to be with him

But he was Anchored to the city

her plane was taking off from.

                                                    He was the departure gate

                                                        delaying her arrival time.

What They Both Agreed

He wanted to say he got the girl

But he couldn't

She wanted to say she loved this boy

But she didn't

They wanted to believe loving each other

Would feel like breathing

But instead

It felt like

Drowning

Except

Without the water.

And there's a word for that

They called it suffocating.

They both agreed

this would be the worst

Way to live

This feeling of dying

Like two bugs drawn to the fumes

of a freshly coated wall of paint

Accidentally caught

stuck

Dying in the drying

Window pane

Would that pain

Be but brutal for the bugs.

Dying is never easy

When we're designed to stay alive

Bodies built to last

Hearts meant for beating

for ever

For each other

But they both agreed:

slow deaths

& long goodbyes

Are amongst the worst forms of human torture.

Playing With Fire

Must have been the lesson they taught

The day we skipped Home Economics

Even after all these years

We still haven't learned

How this might be

Hazardous to our health.

If a boy walks away from a girl

and no one is around to stop him

Is she still abandoned?

Bedside Manner

He is the night howler

outside the windows of her soul

Tearing at the nightmares she keeps reliving

Howling a broken hallelujah

at her full moon innocence

Preying a dear girl like her would love a carnivore like him

He prays she lets him in

He makes deals with the night sky for her body

And sends her bedtime stories

riddled with lies

Before her dream catchers can catch them

But she knows better

Knows that boys who kiss girls

without permission are not the heroes

They are the wolves lurking in the woods

Waiting for the women in red heels

He is not the boy of her dreams

His is the wolf crying boy

at the mercy of her bedside.

Shadow Puppet

He is the shadow puppet

Papi warned us about

When he tucked us in at night

With a forehead kiss

And a subtle good night

That growled against the dying day

& the lingering presence

of any shadow boys

Who lost their way

and might still

be refusing

to grow up.

Liminality

the problem

with being the girl of your dreams

begins when you forget

how to distinguish

between fantasy

and an actual woman

Standing in the room

When you had the opportunity to love me

You chose to keep on dreaming

It is no longer enough.

It should go without saying:

We deserve to be wanted

Without hesitation

& this, of course,

is the very least we deserve.

Metaphors

Since the day they met

She showed her love to him in metaphors

But now it seems that was never enough

Always loving him symbolically

Hiding behind hints

and hyperbolic hypotheticals.

But she did love him

Metaphorically speaking of course

She did love him

She just didn't know how to tell him

Without hiding behind a poem and a rhyme

Her love for him is metaphor.

Always symbolizing so much more

than she could ever piece together in a poem

or quantify with words.

Hyperbole

She tried to disarm him.

He who needed body armor

Just to say hello.

She didn't try to deceive him.

She simply used metaphors to make meaning

For feelings she couldn't easily admit to feeling.

She loved him

in more metaphors than she ever thought possible.

Each one symbolic

of whatever sacred thing

they held between them.

But metaphors are only minor attempts

to describe what's real

but their magic exists only in what they mirror

Beautiful Illusions we refuse to break.

Rent

Some days he still thinks of her

But these thoughts are uninvited guests.

She moves like an illegal jaywalker

crossing his mind without permission

Some nights she is the monster beneath his bed

That's chosen to live rent free inside his head,

But this poem is her eviction notice.

Every memory of her slowly vacating

As the boy begins to dream again

To ease his mind

and rest his restless heart again.

Conversations In The Shade

He spoke

And she listened

Careful not to confuse his first language

with his tribal identity.

What can cure a broken heart?

Perhaps the dreams we dream by day?

Or the poetry we write by night?

Eternal Childhood Of An Escapist Mind

She was tired

of being Peter Pan's pipe dream

a muse for the boys who refused to grow old

He grew into the sort of adult who still waited around for the

ice cream trucks

While she learned to tuck her shadow beneath her pillowcase

and push away any dreams of

growing old together

Girl taught boy to turn his night terrors into daydreams

While boy made girl feel forever young

She is an old soul while he is a kid at heart

Unable to live without the other

They rely on imagination to survive

Tethering themselves to worlds far richer than reality

They lived inside their heads

Perfecting the art of dreaming during the day

They cultivated lands where time remains unplanned

And in the end,

It was their love,

That made them both immortal.

Dreamland

Can we put "the dream" in quotations for now?

They sold us a notion we all bought

And paid full price for

No refunds or exchanges

We put our sleep on hold for now

Can we wake up to the truth for now?

That not all dreams are created equal

Not all dreams are meant for dreaming

Some dreams are a fantasy

A fallacy we invest in

With no guarantee for our deposit

Can we put "the dream" into quotations for now?

Because no amount of recall will bring back the dream

we all once dreamt when sweetest slumber knew our name.

I Want To Reclaim Language

until painful,
demoralizing,
and dehumanizing
words have taken back enough power
to give us life again.

I want to reclaim my body
until Innocence,
boundaries,
and birthrights
are restored to me.

I want to reclaim my existence in this skin
until generational traumas are undone
in my bones
In my veins
In my lungs
and oxygen can bring me peace again.

I want to reclaim what eyes have seen
before my vision was distorted
and imagination stolen.
Before my clarity was clouded
and we paid full price for a dream that cost them nothing
in exchange for nightmares that only keep us up at night.

I want to reclaim everything
Demand for restitutions
Until the return on investment is so great
That it gives rest to the restless.

That Night

He asked her two questions about God.
When she answered both questions he was surprised to
learn she had given him the same answer for both.

At first he asked her:
"What do you believe to be true about God?"
To which she responded, "Almost everything I've heard."

Then he asked her,
"What do you struggle to believe about God?"
To which she responded, "Almost everything I've heard."

Before leaving she said to him:
"Some days relationship with God
Feels more like a wrestling match.

and some nights, that wrestling will keep you up at night."

He tried to understand how *this too*
could be faith.

That night, they both stayed up addressing their questions to
the sky
until the Sun came up in the morning.

re·al·ized
/ˈrē(ə)ˌlīzd/

verb
a dream come true experienced while in the state of wakefulness

Campfires & Storytelling

When I found out I could make a living telling stories

I wanted to tell our story first.

Corn, Cactus, Turtle
after Gloria Anzaldúa

Sometimes, we take our culture in by the spoonfuls.
Some bites easier to swallow than others
But we chew nonetheless
For the reminder that there is still something to take in
Some richness to taste
Some history to thank
Some flavor, some rhythm, some traditional pattern of hand movements
And ingredients
Passed down from abuelita's kitchen
Something to hold on to.

Sometimes we take our culture in by the mouthful.
Too much to wrap our head and hearts around so we open up our mouths
And try to take in as much memory as our native tongues will allow
In one single breath we pass down story after story of who we are
And where we come from
And what we eat
And how we dance
Because our culture is one of ancient oral tradition where
Every spoonful counts

Whether it is a shout, or song, or el sancocho de mama
We don't let it get away from us
We open our mouths wide
As if every bit of our existence depended on this feeding
On this knowledge
On this feeding of our knowledge
And we bite down *real* hard

Trying our best not to let go, not to forget, not to forsake, not to deny, not to ever do anything
other than always remember exactly where you came from nina
Because *this*, spoonful of bread from mama mija, is the substance of life.
And someday, we'll put so much platano and tortilla, in your body that your veins will
identify this as your lifeline, your bloodline, your blood type:
L for Latina Positive
No matter what they tell you when you walk out these doors
There is nothing negative about you

So here eat your food
And try to hold in as much steam as you can
Never letting the heat make you bitter
Never let the hatred make you angry
Don't burn your tongue on swallowed pride,
No wear that pride in your hair like flowers from el campo
So they never forget that while we get our heritage passed down to us in fragments
There is nothing fragmented about us
While we get our history retold to us in pieces
There is nothing broken about where we come from
And while we have to sit and wait for mama and papa to feed us our collective identity by the spoonfuls
There is nothing tasteless about us
A good meal takes time
A great understanding of who we are
and where we come from
takes even more time

So I will not rush papa when he tells me about

Los mayas, los incas, y los taínos
I will not hurry mama when she looks me in the eyes on
the first day of every school year
To remind me that I am beautiful
Buckets of curls and all
That there is a place for me
That I am not merely pretty for a dark-skinned girl
That I am gorgeous even when I am not their standard
of straight-haired blue-eyed beauty
That I am more than a "foreign-form-of-attractive" or an
"exotic-type-of beauty"
That I am more than *different* pretty

I will not rush my mother when she tries to open a space
I mean force a space for me in society
Because someday I will need that space
I will stand in the [head] space between "good food"
and "not good-enough" identity
And I will be grateful that mami took her time with me
That she did HER BEST to brush
every bit of doubt
Every ounce of insecurity
Any chance of confusion that caught itself on these
tightly coiled curls
Negrita, prieta, morena, mulata
Because it taught me not to be afraid of something that
might someday be used against me
It taught me to embrace the parts of myself that I might
someday come to hate
It forced me not to tear myself from a history, a culture,
a heritage, an inheritance
Of darkness and dance
midnight magic
Of golden beauty and natural hair
      They taught me not to *tear* myself.

        Not to crucify the curls that make up my crown
        Or resent the melanin that makes up my skin
        Or curse the full moon midnight that dwells up my eyes
    They taught me not to *tear* myself

Mastika mija, my mom would tell me,
You have to learn to eat
To take in whatever is put on the table for you and
Find the nutritional value in everything
If you don't like something -- articulate it well
Without an accent in your mouth
Or salsa and chile still hidden underneath the breath of your untamed tongue
Mija, papa advices, make sure if you do speak you make us proud
Our culture is one of open wounds that we cannot surgically attend to
So when you speak make sure it sounds like healing
Tastes like nurture and feels like hope
Make sure you open more doors than you close
And when they slam you out because you are more alien than ally
Make sure you identify all the possible worlds within each wound First
And treat every wall they built against you like it is Jericho and not Border
You can always march around (God non-violence)
And just give it time
But never stop believing
Because believing we overcome, is what makes us overcome
So da gracias to the hands that feed you
And always, mija, *pray before you eat.*

XYZ

When my niece was born

I knew right away

She was the metaphor

I'd been trying to write down for years.

Childhood Homes

Reptilians shed their skin

While caterpillars blossom into butterflies

Humans evolve as well

Though we often forget to thank

The cocoon that nested us

all those years we journeyed about

in our process of becoming

Driving Lessons
for Papi

When Papi taught me how to drive
He simultaneously offered me a valuable life lesson.

I remember he said, "Never look down at the road right in front of you. This will throw you off. You're moving so fast that what's right in front of you will be right behind you before you know it. Instead, visualize where you want to go. Look up ahead. Keep your eyes on the road and see where you want the vehicle to go because wherever you are looking is where you will eventually
end up."

I never forgot that lesson.

I didn't know it at the time
But my father was giving me the secret to life.

Melanin

We live in a world where the voice of the earth can
swallow us whole

Holes meant to swallow us
silence our holiness and
convince us that we are not wholly dust

Fully human
Not enough

The earth tried to swallow her up
But She took her fist to the ground
until the pounding of her heart broke open galaxies
even the moon could not eclipse

Black hole tried to swallow her whole until she looked it
dead in the eye, whispered:

"Hold me.

I'm not afraid of you. I'm from you. Swallow me whole
and I'll break free over and over
again like a shooting star racing home after dark.

I am midnight and magic,

Moonbeam, and madness.

The product of your pool.

I am the untold story of your deepest,

darkest magnetic pull."

Roam and the American Passport

I was traveling from the U.S. to Rome.

On my way back from Ireland,

Mami calls to ask if I made it safely past customs

I tell her everything went smoothly, as always.

To which Mami responds,

"Ay mija, si supieras que ese es el lujo de viajar con un pasaporte americano."

"Oh my daughter, if only you knew that is the luxury of traveling with an American passport."

Margins

When I see a blank page I see possibility

My eyes are immediately drawn to the margins

Because it is in the margins where I do some of my best

work

I have always been the sort of person to color outside of

the lines

Because outside of the lines

Is where the magic happens

When we make our home within the margins

We conquer borders

That once held us back,

but now set us free.

So when they call me

and my people

"marginalized"

I almost always hear it as a compliment.

Family. Friends.

and the familiar.

these alone feel like

divinity on earth.

Colocha
for Mami

She is the one who went to Beauty School
Who learned to cut and braid and style curls
Much like her own,
Yet different from her own.

For Mami,
Who gave us kinks, taught us to detangle
and who also helped us with our hair.

For Hairdresser,
Who did so much more than dress our hair.

For Mami,
who made magic with our locks and braided prayers
into our hair
while teaching us the art of self love for curly hair.

Past Tense

Missing requires memory
To miss, is to remember
Thinking is solely intellectual
Whereas missing
and remembering
require deep emotional synthesis that simply does not
take place in the mind
Missing takes place in the heart
Missing is the aching of the heart
The yearning of a soul that has been split
Missing should feel, in part, like endless, unrequited
desire

Missing is longing,
but requires the rememory of the past
Remembering things as they were
Not romanticizing them as they were not

Thus re-memory becomes the lifeblood of moving
forward
                              moving on
                                    and
                              letting go

Missing is about learning the lessons of the loss feeling
the bruises of the break up and healing
from the trauma of the heartbreak

Sometimes all that's missing is, is bandaging the aches
and gluing gold around the cracks
Sometimes all that missing is, is asking the heart
where it hurts and using alchemy
to mend our worn and clay-cracked souls

To mend the split in our psyche by
Re-entering the painful past itself
So I hope you miss me
Not because I hope you hurt
But because I pray you heal.

Surviving, Surviving

She is not lost.
Nor is she losing.

She may have suffered a loss,
but she is far from losing.

She is the sort of fighter that's better known as a survivor.
She is the sort of wanderer that is never lost,
yet always found.

It just so happens that, for her,
this is what surviving looks like.

Isn't it great how we can sense emotion based on tone?

Yet why can't we communicate the bad feelings as

eloquently

or graciously as we communicate the good ones?

Growth Spurt

She stayed and forgave

until finally her love for self

outgrew her love for him and others.

Para Mis Abuelos

Para Abuelo
El cual me enseñó a andar en bicicleta y todavía recorre conmigo el sendero costero del amanecer al atardecer

Para Abuela
La cual me dio amor, protección, vestidos rojos, y ojos que siempre me vieron por quien realmente soy una y otra vez

Para Abuelo
El cual me dio a mi padre, una pasión agricultora, y nos enseñó a amar esta bella tierra de Dios

Para Abuela
La cual tiene más fuerza y amor en sus dos ojos de lo que jamás creí posible y la cual siempre demuestra su fe inquebrantable

Para los ancianos, *mis* ancianos
Que nunca han faltado un cumpleaños
Los que siempre me llamán
Y los cuales me aman profundamente

Sin ustedes, nada de esto sería posible.

For My Grandparents

For Abuelo
Who taught me how to ride a bike and still rides the coastal trail with me sunrise to sunset

For Abuela
Who gave me love, protection, poofy red dresses, and eyes that saw for who I really am time after time

For Abuelo
Who gave me my father, a green thumb, and taught us to love God's green earth

For Abuela
Who holds more strength and love in her eyes than I ever thought possible and is the epitome of unwavering faith

For the ancianos, MY ancianos
Who never miss a birthday
Who always call
And who love me deeply

Without you, none of this is possible.

Writer's Block

You inspire me

You draw poetry out of me

Which isn't always the case.

Most people give me writer's block.

But not you.

For now,

This is all I know.

Gravity

She broke his heart

While simultaneously teaching him so much

about love and loss and every bittersweet feeling of

falling that exists in-between.

Make Poetry Great Again

I want to go back
Back to when poets didn't feel need to be activists all the time
When we didn't always write for the sake of a movement
But instead we wrote because something moved us

Back to when poetry was just about poetry
When a muse could be as simple as a butterfly in your stomach
or something as human as heartbreak
I miss the days when basic human connections were all we wrote about
But now we hold our poetry up with picket signs and parade our platforms through our pieces
partly because we feel we need to give the people what they want, in this case it's a voice,
and partly because we feel we have to

All things considered though we kind of have to, no?
I mean take me for example:
A Latinx female with curls and curves..
So to some extent I am expected to write *that poem* right?
To some extent I have to talk about being brown
Or being thick
Or being both and insecure
Right?
I mean Du Bois said it best when he wrote about double-consciousness
I want to go back
Back to when W.E.B. Du Bois, one of the greatest writers in the American canon, wrote *The Souls of Black Folk* and broke down his own struggle with this very dilemma

I mean what is one to do?
We owe it to our people to represent
Owe it to the people to tell our story
Owe it to this country.. I guess.. to be "mutant & proud"
or something I am not sure
You can't be brown and write about much else
You can't be queer and talk about much else
It doesn't matter if you're brilliant, gorgeous, talented,
and fabulous
Mandela said
& Du Bois knew it too
If you're an artist of any kind than you're an activist by
trade
To be anything less might be a disservice
But what about poetry?

I want to go back
To Shihan at Def Jam reciting his famous "This Type
Love" love lines
To a time when poets wrote about love and all was right
in the world
When love poems weren't a cliché they were standard
poetry
Like a rite of passage for any writer's coming of age

I want to go back
Back to when love poems were about real love
    deep love
        that walk 500 hundred miles
            just to walk a thousand miles type
            love
I mean my dad actually *did that* for my mom
Back in the day when he was in basic for the Marines
He used to walk two miles
10,560 feet
Almost one hour each way

Just to get to the phone where he would call my mom
for approximately ten minutes
Long distance
Only to walk him back another two miles
10,560 feet
For an additional one hour's time

Nowadays I know if a guy really likes me because he
turns on his messaging notifications
on IG just to get the alert that I'm even reaching out

And love becomes nothing more than a series of back
and forth ellipses

I tell my dad this story and he doesn't understand the
men... or better yet the boys... of my
generation
I tell him neither do I

I want to go back
To a time when love was simpler and heartbreak was
less frequent

To a time when you couldn't just ghost someone because
there was no technology enabling
your avoidant behavior

To a time when we risked our lives for love
Racing to pick up the phone because you gave a boy
your landline number and you had to
answer the phone before daddy picked up the line

To a time when love was inspirational & breathtaking

Worth sneaking out in the middle of the night because
even though I still got curfew this

might be real love and that makes this worth it

I want to go back
To a time when love still moved us
To a time when boys walked miles just to call us back
To a time when love was worth our time
And our poetry of course
But with our modern-day-watered-down-romance it's no wonder poets write more about
movements than about a love that does or doesn't move us
All I'm saying is: thanks for the memories.
      Thanks for the poems,
           the inspirations,
                the good times,
                    and the examples.
                        — Thanks for the standards
                            I want to go back
                                wayyy back

We Spend So Much Time

thinking about making the right or wrong decisions
when it comes to our love lives
But the thing about love and life
is that there truly is no such thing as right or wrong
when it comes to life or love

At the end of the day there's only the choices we
make And the lives we are left to live with.

There
is
nothing
more
frustrating
than
having
found
the
words
in
Spanish,
but
having
no
English
equivalent
for
translation

Citing Sources

She told him
How she loved him
But she forgot to
Cite her sources

Each time she said "I love you"
She quoted from past lifetimes
With past lovers

Though her heart could never plagiarize
The way she felt about him.

Even though her lips were citing sources
Her heart had started writing vows.

A Few Good Men

To the men who hold us with their bare hands
Who embrace us with their full arms and say we fill them fully
Making us feel fulfilled, to these men, who heal us truly
To the men who use words like:
Perfect
Gorgeous
Special
And Enough
when talking about us
When talking *to* us
To the men who look us in the eyes when they make love to us
To the men who come after the man that "loved us"
but then "left us" when he said that we were "less than"
To the men who teach us that love is spelled with *you* at the end
Who show us that love is written only in Present tense
That love never comes with a question mark at the end
To the men that treat us as though we are more answers than we are questions marks
To the men who do not use us to heal themselves or quench their thirst for sensuality
Who do not use our bodies to build their egos on
Or our hearts to shape their pride on
Or treat us as altars to pray their sins away
to the men who fill our headspace with more worship than repentance

To the men who are more answered prayer than they are question marks
Whose punctuation is a graceful accent to our already complete sentences

To the men who treat us like we are already complete sentences

To the men who teach us a different love. and better care
To the men who don't get enough credit
Who know a little bit about everything
Who love every curve and handful of us well rounded women
To the men who just sit and watch us while we perform mundane tasks as though we are the
most exquisite of things in all existence
To the men that will hold us when we tell them how another man broke us
To the man who doesn't man handle a broken heart but mends hearts by holding *us* with his
bare hands.

She Was The Type

of lover that would make you green eggs and ham for

breakfast.

She made everything magical,

even mundane things like breakfast.

Loving her was more surreal than anything

because she made living feel like dreaming.

How many jobs does it take

to get to the center of the American dream?

If People Were Poetry

I think if people were poetry you would be my favorite poem
My nephew would probably be a sonnet of some sort
& my older sister would be written in iambic pentameter I'm sure
Something rhythmic, slightly musical
Yet orderly & restrained, but well rounded, not at all contained
You on the other had would be the sort of poem I would definitely put music behind
Something soulful and jazzy or
Underground Rhythm & Blues
The kind of poem that would sound well string instruments or percussion
Or snaps and room full of silent souls
If people were poetry
I think Dad would be that Spanish Pablo Neruda poem
I'd read en la sala bajo una luz
apagada
Mami would be extensive poem… that cross between "writer's block" and a flood of
inspiration.
That poem I'm excited to start and dreading to finish
My niece, like a xylophone perfectly in tune, would be less of a poem and more of a
Dr. Seuss riddle with poetic resemblance
My younger niece would be a more complex piece, deep as the sea, she is wild & free
Like an Emily Dickinson poem, she'd be a "wounded deer leaps the highest" sort of poem
Nothing like my younger sister who would be the sort of poem that would rhyme and easily
make sense … but maybe not always… not so easily.

Straightforward at first, but in an elegant … not so simple … underrated sort of way

But I swear if people were poetry you would be my favorite poem
Everything about you
Like a metaphor I can't quite wrap my head around
Or your smile the simile I can't quite balance all my likes on
You personify my entire world
Nothing getting lost in translation
I get every reference that you are
Your puns all perfectly intended
Each punchline perfectly delivered
You are so much more than that one fire line in the middle of the poem
You are the whole grand slam
And you are worth not editing
I'd love you just the way you are
Re-reading each line over and over again as though it was the first time
Because there are layers of intrigue behind each one of your lines
& I am bound by the familiarity of your words & the comfort of knowing I already know
your content which makes us both content

If people were poetry I think you & I would rhyme
or we'd sound alike
or synchronize in the sort of way that *accentuates*
Complementing, but not distracting
We are not a distraction
Wouldn't hold each other back either
We'd be more like that run on sentence that would go on forever

They say a poem is never finished it is only abandoned,
and I know that if people were poetry
and you were a poem
I would never give up on you.

Pelo Malo?

We all have different hair

Mami a soft curl

Papi a kinky coil

Hermana mayor a loose twist

Me a tight texture

Baby sister a short wave

Abuelo now bald

Pero en el barrio,
but in the barrio

La vecindad de su niñez,
the neighborhood of his childhood

They still call him Colocho
Spanish for curly

Life insists on our undivided attention.

Each morning this life begging to be lived

wakes us up from sleeping

and anything that demands

more attention than our dreams

at the very least

deserves our full attention.

I am

The next time someone asks me if I'm mixed,

I will tell them that I am.

I am a mix of my mother and my father.

Daughter of immigrants and dreamers,

Soy mezcla de Mami y Papi.

What If

What if I want more than

Simple mind games?

What if I want 'live and in color'?

What if I want to be loved in the flesh,

Not just feel it in my bones?

I want wind-chime love

Wake me up in the middle of the night love

The sort of love that kisses my cheek

like moonlight

but warms me up

like sunlight

What if I want the sort of love that wakes me up,

like sunrise,

Forces me out of a dream

Keeps me from sleeping and

Forces you to make me more than a fantasy?

What if?

Evolution of a Voice Box

When I was five years old I learned to hold my voice like
a box of crayons
Learned to pick and choose the colors and tones I'd want
to paint the world with
I learned to appreciate the softer tones
so I was certain the world would hear me

In high school I learned to hold my voice like a love note
To pass it around quietly and secretly in the hallways
with the ones I loved
Who also loved me back
This is how I learned that a voice
could be sacred
That words could hold secrets
That pen and paper are often
the best means of communication
That I could say a lot with
a rhyme and a metaphor for love
That people would listen if I talked about love
So I passed love notes instead of hate notes

Learning to hold my voice like a pinky promise, I'd fold
into a paper airplane
And send off to the first person I'd trust
This is how I learned that a voice
could be given away
That a voice could contain power,
not just information:

The first time I learned to say no
I held my voice like a stop sign
& learned that it actually works
The first time I said I'm sorry
I held my voice like a white flag

The first time I said goodbye
I held my voice like a semi-colon
unsure of where to place it
The first time they couldn't say it back
I turned my voice into a run-on sentence
that I yelled into the pages of my notebook
and I called it my first poem
The first time I said I like you
I held my voice like a key I wanted to put back in my
pocket

The next time I said I love you too
I held my voice like a mirror with too many cracks to see
anything real reflected back
The first time I told someone I didn't love them anymore
my voice turned into a heavy suitcase filled with more
things than I could carry
The last time I said yes to someone
I held my voice like a penny at a wishing well knowing I
only get an answer if I learn how to
let go so I threw my voice in and it came back like an
echo

At home I was taught to hold my voice like a maraca
AND a machete
My parents raised daughters who learned
to sings songs like battle cries
& who wailed their war cries into melodies

I learned my voice held the power of life & death

I learned this from a God who created galaxies with the
power of His poetry

A voice isn't meant to be something

We carry hidden
Tucked away in the back pocket
Of our least favorite jeans

However, when the officer stops me on the corner of
Ingra & 14th Avenue,
Asks for my license & registration
I not only wonder how he carries his voice,
But I notice I am shaking

For the first time since the first grade I hold my voice out like a question mark
Like a hymn, or a prayer, or a confession of sins I have forgotten the words to
& now present at the altar of someone else's mercy

Most days I hold my voice like a megaphone
But tonight I hold my voice out like a coffee mug filled with too much black tea

Worried, I hope he hears my voice like a road map held between the two of us
leading us BOTH back home safely

I think of my parents back home
My father: a pastor who plays guitar
My mother: a preacher who plays bass
Both parents taught me
to hold my voice like instrument
Told me to carry it with two good hands
Showed me how to use it from a pulpit
Prophetically & unafraid

But tonight
I am terrified

Tonight my voice is more *acoustic than electric*
Tonight my voice is not defense mechanism
Tonight it feels like a weapon
I can only conceal, but not carry

Hesitantly I hold my voice like water
slipping through my fingers

This is now survival of the quietest

Some days I hold my voice out like a firecracker and
dismiss it into the night sky
and watch as it marries one or more stars
But tonight I am afraid that firecrackers
Can be mistaken for firearms
So instead I wear my voice
like a bullet proof vest and sit still

The officer asks a few questions
and checks my information
When he returns
He lets me go
Not even a warning
Just a simple "drive safe miss"
and a subtle tap to the car

When he first pulled up I asked myself
how might a man like him hold his voice
I notice / know now
How he, too, holds it like a question mark

Like a stop sign
Like white flag
Like a penny at a wishing well
& a roadmap home

I wonder, then, who taught him
not to hold it like an echo?

Driving away
I am grateful.
I hold my voice like a gift
Like a caged bird being set free
I sing
I sing
I sing

Old Soul

Eternity is a timeless poet, begging to be experienced.

We are the ones who keep running out of paper.

Los Ancianos Soñarán Sueños

Dreaming is in my blood

Before I was the daughter of immigrants

I was the daughter of dreamers

Born into a lineage of

men and women

who dream dreams

Who turn children into visionaries

And make prophets out of poets.

Fire Breather
this poem is for the ones who have ever needed to adapt to their environment in order to survive — also for Mami y Papi whose own survival has made mine possible

She is no houseplant.

She is untamed wildflower

She requires no attention

Or artificial intentions

She thrives better in free light

She is wide open spaces

Without warning

Trigger, gunfire, recoil

All in one

She is the fireweed that grew from

volcanic ash and bonfire embers

She is survival embodied in a dreamer

Fire-breathing female

She became the ring of fire they tried to scorch her with.

10 Lessons My Curls Have Taught Me

1. The best things in life are wild and free

2. We don't need relaxers because we're not stressed out

3. There is no such thing as taming what is designed to be uninhibited

4. What God sets free, is free indeed

5. Stubbornness and resistance is in our genes: the gift of our parents, the pride of our tribe.

6. Accept yourself. Love yourself. Kinks and all

7. We're designed with purpose. Messy isn't always messy

8. Every kink + coil is meant to be seen, loved, appreciated, and most importantly liberated

9. Flaws are okay. Some days there will be flyaways and other days every curl and aspect of life will fall

perfectly in place. Both are out of your control, yet both are divine.

10. Flow with the process which ebbs and flows. This is natural. Learn to embrace natural, which in our case, also ebbs and flows

Becoming

The question should not be:
Which outcome do I want?
But rather: *At the end of this, who do I wish to be?*

What version of myself can I be most proud of?
What is needed next for the evolution of my consciousness?
My healing? My growth? My becoming?

                        These are far greater questions.

Have you ever noticed

how much our peace is dependent

on our capacity for imagination?

Antepasados

After everything her ancestors went through,

She had to believe survival was in her genes.

Dream Recollection

You kept saying

How much you didn't want to lose me,

But then preceded to do nothing

When you finally did.

You kept trying to remember that dream.

Kept forcing yourself back to sleep

Drifting into dreamland because you said

it had something to do with us.

I kept trying to tell you, we could have reality instead.

The Greatest Gift

We can give ourselves

Is the ability to identify behaviors

That create patterns in our lives.

Arrugas & Grey Hair
for mami & papi. The ones who never slept.
The ones for whom I wrote this book. Gracias por el sueño, the one I'm living now.

Sometimes I think we think we're going to live forever

I went off to school
I learned lots
Unlearned more
Found myself
Came back home
And found there have been more fights
With Mami & Papi than I ever remember having before

It is as though with every fight
I notice more and more grey hairs on my father's head
& the wrinkles in my mother's face

I analyze
and think about
All the ones that I have put there...

The grey hairs in my father's beard
put there with every 6am drive to work as he put me through school
The wrinkles I gave Mami
with every phone call from school or pink slip or letter from teacher because
I was chronically late or absent on my own accord
The wrinkles I gave Mami from issues with boys or nights out too late
The grey hairs I gave Papi from talking back or being too much like him

The other day I didn't see my parents for a whole day

An entire 24 hours

And that night when I saw my father heading off to bed
Looking at the back of his head all I noticed were his
grey hairs

Fixated,
All I could think was how many of those did I put there?

How many more nights will I kiss Papi buenas noches
and watch as he goes off to bed
With crown of stress & silver splendor leading him off to
sleep
All because of a dream, *un sueño ahora realizado,*
That Papi and Mami gave to me.

gratitude

There are so many people I wish to thank. If I were now to list the names of all who have supported, mentored, loved, and/or inspired me I am certain I would be the one running out of paper. Please know, from the bottom of my soul, how deeply grateful I am to love and be loved by you. With that said, I will do my best to be both thorough and concise.

a mis padres, Moyce y Sara. mi faro. mi ancla. sus sueños han regado con agua la tierra de la cual continúo floreciendo. su amor y sacrificio siguen siendo mis olas de rescate. yo soy, porque ustedes son.

to my sisters, Tai Tai and Es. my teachers. my shadowboxers. my guardians. you are sunrays and precipitation and all the good things that make heaven touching earth feel real and possible. my melody is incomplete without our three part harmony. thank you for always agreeing to dance.

a mis abuelos, a toda mi tribu. ni inspiración divina. con un solo sueño y su amor sin reservas me han puesto el mundo entero a mi alcance. gracias por sus sacrificios. su revolución vive infinitamente en la tinta de mis dedos.

to my poetry family. my muses. my drum circle. may these pages fuse our revolution.

to my professors. Mr. Moyer*, Sra. Liranzo*, Mr. Dvorak*, Dr. Schaak*, Dr. Hintze-Pothen*, Jill Neimeyer, Jeremiah Peck, Rob Hildebrand, and Dr. Lawless. my mirrors. my sounding boards. your lessons have influenced both my writing and my character. thank you for guiding me and believing in my voice. *English, Spanish, or literary professors*

to my dear soulmates. more than friends. my nucleus. my pockets of home. you've seen me grow, cry, leave before I get left, cry some more, heal, progress, and have accepted every single one of my apologies. thank you for staying. you are oceans and oceans of depth and beauty.

to my dearest Swan. my best friend. you are honey and promise and humility personified. thank you for my amazing cover art and for always holding space. your love is the deepest exhale.

to Emerson. you are warmest candlelight. thank you for your honest feedback + endless support.

to my nieces and nephew, Xyla, Elliot, & Zoe. my heart centers. divine sages. thank you for enriching my life. you teach me so much about life and love, I hope someday to return the favor.

to God. my source. my everything. you are the poetry and the Poet. my wholehearted gratitude.

to The Voices Project. my answered prayer. thank you for this incredible opportunity. for valuing my sacred stories and giving my poetry a permeant place in this world.

last but not least, to YOU, my readers. my old souls. my fellow nomads. you have given this book a home. thank you for caring, for accepting my invitation, for feeling every emotion alongside me while experiencing your own journey. thank you for understanding. I am honored you took time to merge your path with mine. thank you for reading, always.

About the Author

Raquel Polanco is a Hispanic-American poet in her mid-twenties who is continually inspired by God, humpback whales, tall trees, Jupiter, and castles made of sand. Her roots can be traced back to Mayan and Taino ancestors through her father and mother's Dominican and Honduran origins.

Born and raised in Anchorage, Alaska Raquel became an avid speaker and prolific writer within her community and throughout the PNW. Graduating with her BA in English and Theology, she continued to use storytelling as her main form of advocacy and self-expression. She centers most of her writing around the politics of culture, gender, spirituality, depth of emotions, heartache, and the essence of human interconnectedness. She believes storytelling holds the power to unify humanity thus she does her best to write with as much honesty and introspection as paper allows pen.

Raquel currently resides in Portland, OR where she spends her down time daydreaming, hammocking, and exploring with her pup Zuko — all the while writing poetry in her head. Poetry is, for her, the sacred path towards healing and empathy.

Made in the USA
Monee, IL
01 November 2021